BEYOND POPCORN

A CRITIC'S GUIDE TO LOOKING AT FILMS

John Travolta, Uma Thurman in *Pulp Fiction (1994)*.

BEYOND POPCORN

A CRITIC'S GUIDE TO LOOKING AT FILMS

BY

ROBERT GLATZER

EASTERN WASHINGTON UNIVERSITY PRESS
SPOKANE, WASHINGTON

All photos courtesy of Photofest

Library of Congress Cataloging-in-Publication Data
Glatzer, Robert
        Beyond Popcorn: A Critic's Guide to Looking at Films / by
Robert Glatzer
p. cm.
Includes index.
ISBN 0-910055-70-x
 1. Film criticism. 2. Motion pictures. I. Title.

PN1995.G54 2001
791.43'01'5--dc21

                                        00-067745

Cover design by Scott Poole
Book design by Joelean Copeland
Author photo by Mickey McKay

For Mary Ann

CONTENTS

INTRODUCTION

When we think about going to a movie these days and look for a little professional help in choosing one, we pick our way through a maze of stars and thumbs, smiley-faces and frowns, diamonds and turkeys, little men on stepladders, icons of videocassettes, and numbers from one to five. Did the film get two stars or three? What about those halves? Is the icon of a video-cassette (wait till it comes out on tape) better or worse than the frowny face? And have the media thought about what to do for icons as DVDs replace those cassettes? It's a hard life, thinking about what to see.

So how do we choose? Maybe the better question is how does a critic choose? Every morning network TV show has a house critic, every magazine, every daily newspaper either has its own or runs a review by a syndicated critic, and every cable TV channel that shows films has a host who's happy to share bits of inside gossip about who did what to whom during the shoot.

Anyway, what do critics know? Often, a lot. Sometimes, not very much. If you took a college course in Movies 101, you might have seen two films a week for a semester, and you wrote about them on the final. If you were lucky, your teacher knew what he or she was talking about; if not, you got the English professor who just liked to show off. If after college you should find yourself connected to films in one way or another, you will be amazed at the extremes of knowledge and ignorance you find around you. Let me give you an example: In 1998 the American Film Institute, an organization devoted to the heritage of film, decided to ask fifteen hundred movie professionals (the list was confidential but included studio executives, craft and creative types, theatre owners and others) to name their choices as the 100 best American films of all time from a list of 400 the Institute had prepared. The plan was that the film that got the most mentions would be 'the best,' the film with the second most would be made number 2, and so on. They offered three criteria for the choices: historical significance; critical recognition and awards; and popularity as measured by box office grosses, syndication receipts, and video sales and rentals. The event caused much consternation, and infuriated many critics, because a) no one could agree on just what those criteria meant; b) the criteria themselves had little to do with what we think of as a film's artistic quality; and c) they took the individual respondent's own reactions completely out of play. Do bigger grosses mean a better film? Is George Lucas a better filmmaker than Ingmar Bergman? You see where this leads.

So let's forget about stars and numbers for a moment and think about where movies stand in relation to the other arts. The arts are pretty much everywhere in our lives. We read novels because their authors' inventions have something to say to us; we respond to paintings because the artist's work gives us esthetic and sometimes intellectual pleasure; we listen to music because it appeals to our emotions and our intellect at the same time; but an awful lot of us go to a movie for reasons that have nothing to do with quality. We go because it's a way to spend a couple of hours. It's better than the mall, or it's at the mall, or it's exciting or romantic or sexy, or the theatre has good popcorn, or our date wants to go, or it's the only film we can take the kids to, or about a thousand other reasons that have nothing to do with the quality of the movie itself. And we don't know, or care, who, if anybody, made it, nor how or why it was made.

This is not a book about who made certain films, but it is built around the idea that movies are an art form and that good artists make better movies than bad ones. That's not a revolutionary thought, but the message doesn't seem to have taken hold among a lot of filmgoers. Somehow movies are too ubiquitous in our lives to generate much critical consideration. Hollywood studios traditionally have made films as 'entertainment' rather than as works of 'art,' and any art in the work was just a little bonus and not to be overvalued. But all arts consist of works deliberately crafted and structured to communicate to the viewer or listener or reader some intellectual and emotional message, hopefully with power and wit and insight, so that the recipient emerges from that confrontation with a better understanding of him or herself and the world he or she lives in.

That's art, and it lets us begin with the premise that every film is a work of art, good or bad. This book will look at a number of films and see them as a critic sees them. We'll go into some detail about the elements that make up a movie: the writing, direction, acting, shooting, and editing. We'll also deal with larger constructs like comedy, film musicals, and the differences between foreign and American films. This is not a text, but it will give you language to describe the films you see, the background to understand what works and what doesn't; and an acquaintance with the elements that make a good film better than a bad one. It's a book for anybody who wants to think about films, talk about them, and treat them as examples of an art form rather than just as momentary entertainments.

That's not always easy. Studios have a dreadful impulse to devalue their own work. They've invested many millions of dollars in each film, hired writers to create them, directors to shoot them, and actors, usually stars, to play in them. Then they add millions more to market them. Yet they continue to insist that they're nothing but entertainments, and of course in many cases they're right. Entertainment is fun, but it isn't art all by itself. But sometimes, often against their own best judgment, they will turn out films that are important works of art. The classic example is Paramount's *The Godfather*, which survived more crises in preproduction and production than even the most inventive soap opera writer could ever manage to come up with. The studio didn't want Marlon Brando to play Vito Corleone (too unreliable), didn't want Al Pacino to play Michael (too short — he was referred to as "the midget"), and didn't want Francis Ford Coppola to direct (had made only bad movies). But from the day it opened it's been recognized as one of the great achievements in film history. Chapter 9 of this book will go into some detail about the movie and its value as a work of art.

One area the book doesn't deal with is television. Video — as opposed to television — can be an art form, and many artists today are working in it. But in general television is a medium and not an art. It is a medium for transmitting news, information, sports, and films that were made elsewhere, whether or not they were intended for showing on the air. Prime time series like the currently popular *E.R.* and *The West Wing* for example, are movies made to a television format, with plot or personal conflict 'beats,' or emotional pulses, scheduled for each commercial break, and ongoing characters and plot lines that overlap and stretch like soap operas across the weeks and episodes. (Let's note here that many studio movies are also made with those 'beats' built in, for later convenience in editing when shown on television with commercial breaks.) Live or taped shows, like *Frasier* or *Just Shoot Me*, are stage playlets or sketches that are recorded by multiple video cameras for later viewing. There's nothing wrong with any of that, of course, but very little that's on television today can qualify as video art. Check your cable listings for channels that show movies, though, and you'll be pleasantly surprised at how many interesting films are available. And if you don't live in a major metropolitan area, you can rent or buy thousands of them from mail-order or online houses.

However, an amazing technological revolution is changing the way many films are made: it is the new technology of digital video, and it's having an extraordinary effect on the production of movies. George Lucas plans to shoot his final Star Wars films in video, for screening in theatres equipped for video projection — he will transfer them to film for the others — and other filmmakers have already begun shooting features that way, including Thomas Vinterberg (*The Celebration* — 1999) and Mike Figgis (*Time Code* — 2000). Moreover, it is now possible for any filmmaker to shoot and edit a feature film for less than $10,000 in equipment costs. Digital video is the most important innovation in film since the introduction of sound.

Nevertheless, a movie is still a movie, no matter what the technology is. And if there's any message to this book, it's that the world needs more film critics. Not more professionals, necessarily, but more like you — that critic lurking inside you but hiding behind qualifiers like 'self-conscious' or 'not too sure about saying this' or 'probably wrong but' or all the other phrases that smack of insecurity. And don't equate 'critic' with 'negative' or 'bad' or 'boring' or whatever. The more you know about films, the more you'll enjoy them, and the more good things you'll find in them, even the bad ones. Well, maybe not the bad ones.

BEYOND POPCORN

A CRITIC'S GUIDE TO LOOKING AT FILMS

CHAPTER 1

HOW A CRITIC'S BRAIN WORKS

After exhaustive investigation, it has been found that a critic's brain contains an inordinate number of what might be called taste cells. Not quite like those in the mouth, yet serving the same function, they differentiate between what is delicious and what is not, what is palatable and what must be immediately spit out, and what retains a lasting, even memorable flavor. In the critic's brain a film like *The Maltese Falcon* or *Pulp Fiction* gets a big hello and then stays forever imprinted as a taste to be enjoyed many times over. A film like *It's a Mad, Mad, Mad, Mad World* or *Grand Canyon* causes nausea and a general malaise, often lasting until the next interesting film comes along.

When a critic is faced with a question like, "How could my sister fall in love with an idiot like that?" the correct answer is, 'There's no accounting for taste.' When it comes to movies, though, there IS an accounting for taste, and for all critics it starts with a series of questions. The questions aren't written out or spoken aloud, of course; they're more like the taste memories we call on when we try to identify a new food, for example, or the kinetic memories a pianist has of all those years of five-finger exercises when trying to work out the fingering of a new piece. The critic asks, "Where can I place this film in the library of my brain?" And then, "How can I describe it to someone else?" The questions are designed to help the critic set the film in a context, and then make a value judgment about it.

It's the value judgment that separates the critic from the viewer, the insistence on making choices and holding opinions. Think of the questions as your critical five-finger exercises, and then answer them. They deal with the different things that go into making a movie, things that make it good or bad, and if you follow along they might help focus your own reaction so you respond the way a critic would. Think of a film you saw recently, and try the questions out. Don't sweat it. They work as well for *Porky's XII* as they do for *Hamlet*. Here they are.

Was this movie written by a real human being, as opposed to a group of monkeys chained to the proverbial bank of keyboards? You can tell if at any time while you were watching it you felt an emotion, like sorrow, or exaltation, or rage, or sadness, or utter giddiness that went beyond amusement. Monkeys don't show us their feelings, but good writers do.

HUMAN ❏ MONKEY ❏

Did it have a beginning, a middle, and an end? They don't necessarily have to be in order (*Pulp Fiction* begins and ends in the middle), but a movie, like any artwork, has to begin somewhere, go somewhere, and end somewhere. And it shouldn't be the equivalent of the mystery meat we remember from school. You need to see that there's some kind of structure there.

STRUCTURE ❏ MYSTERY MEAT ❏

Were the characters real people? Did you see yourself in any of them? Or somebody in your family or household? The Simpsons are human beings, although they're just drawn on the screen. The Addams family are not. Scarlett O'Hara is a human being. Charles Foster Kane is a human being. Michael Corleone is a human being. Bruce Wayne is not.

REAL ❏ BRUCE WAYNE ❏

Could you tell there was a director involved? Directors take responsibility for bringing the script to life on the screen. The script indicates who says what to whom, and where they say it, and in what location, and what they're doing while they say it. But it's up to the director to tell the actors how to say it, what emotions to convey, and where to look, stand, and move in every scene. The director is also responsible for the overall rhythm of the movie, deciding where it should move quickly, where it should pause, and so on. We'll get into all that in the chapter called "Who decides where the camera goes?" But your task, should you choose to accept it, is to decide if this film actually shows the director's hand, or alternatively the foot or other portion of the anatomy.

DIRECTOR'S HAND AND BRAIN ❑ DIRECTOR'S FOOT OR BUTT ❑

This is a hard one. Did you learn anything worthwhile from the movie? Like did you get any insights into why your high school boyfriend dumped you? Or why your parents still fight after forty years of marriage? Or why your two best friends each love you but hate each other? Or what keeps you from making a commitment? A good movie has to have a didactic component. That is, it has to teach us something we either didn't know, or refused to learn until now. Otherwise it just evaporates during the credits. A good movie has to leave something, like a burr, stuck to our mind after it's over.

BURR ❑ EVAPORATES ❑

Can you compare this movie with another one, and use words like 'better' and 'worse'? I'll show you what I mean with a couple of films, but you don't have to use these yourself. Just pick two films that seemed to have some things in common. For instance: Was *Goodfellas* better than, the same as, or worse than, *Casino*? They were both about the mob. They had the same director, some of the same actors, and Joe Pesci played a psychopath in each one.

Or try this one: Was Kenneth Branagh's *Hamlet* better or worse than his *Much Ado About Nothing*? He directed both films, from, duh, the same writer. Which one is the better film? How come?

Here are the answers that are not allowed:

a) It just is.
b) I don't know.
c) I liked it.
d) I have a headache and I'm going to the refrigerator for a beer.

Here are a few of the answers that are allowed:

a) *Goodfellas* seemed more tightly plotted than *Casino*, which kind of sprawled all over the place, so *Goodfellas* had a better structure than *Casino*.

b) *Casino* had more interesting characters than *Goodfellas*, so it seemed richer, and there was more for me to think about than there was in *Goodfellas*.

c) Branagh as an actor got more meaning out of his lines in *Hamlet* than he did as Benedick in *Much Ado*, where he couldn't keep up with Emma Thompson in all the scenes they had together.

d) Branagh's intensity level was the same throughout his film of *Hamlet*, so you never got to see any highs or lows, while in *Much Ado* he had a wider range of emotions, and even went from ecstasy to despair.

Any answer that contains the words "more," "better," "less," or "different," or compares one film with another, gives you points as a critic.

USED COMPARATIVES ❏ WENT FOR A BEER ❏

So now we have a little common ground to share when we talk about a movie. We start by agreeing to use the same three points of reference — the writing, the direction, the acting. Every film has these three creative sources. Sometimes one person will both write and direct, and occasionally he or she will act in the film as well. If we think of a film as compared to a novel, there are similarities but of course a crucial difference as well. In a novel the writer is the only creator, and the magic lies in the language. The good novelist uses words on the page so that you find yourself immersed in the lives of characters who exist only in your mind. In films, it takes the writer, director, and however many actors to bring that world alive on screen, but the effect should be the same. Did you respond, in what ways were you affected, where were the film's strengths, and where did you find weaknesses?

Let's take each of the three elements — writing, direction, and acting — and look at them separately. Call it "The Three Part Invention."

Part 1 — The Acting

Pick a film you've seen recently, either in a theatre or at home on video. Start at the easy end: the acting. That's what's up on the screen, after all. Was there anyone in the film whom you identified with? Was he or she like someone you know? Maybe it's a wife in an unhappy marriage. A sister fighting over an inheritance. A son looking for his freedom from a domineering father. A husband/wife fighting a custody case. A business owner facing threats from a protection racket. An executive passed over for a promotion. A fantasist whose dreams aren't coming true.

It wasn't them, you know. They appeared courtesy of the actors who created the roles, the people you met on the screen. Were you involved in their lives? Were you with them from moment to moment? If you identified with at least one character, you should mark down a plus for that film. Lots of movies are entertaining, funny, even touching, but the people on screen just aren't there. They're caricatures, or cartoons, or mythic creatures, which is fine if that's what the film is about, but don't mistake them for real people. Sylvester Stallone went from being an actor, in *Rocky,* to being a caricature (from *Rambo* up to but not including *CopLand*). See Chapter 2, "What's the difference between acting and acting in films?" for more discussion of this.

In recent years, there's been an interesting change in movies, particularly Hollywood movies. Producers and studios are casting actors in leading roles who never would have been used before. These are actors who are not known for one screen persona, like Schwarzenegger or Stallone or John Wayne, but are able to create different characters for each film, based on what the writer has given them to work with. Sean Penn, Meryl Streep, Frances McDormand, Jodie Foster, Kevin Spacey, Denzel Washington, and James Woods come to mind. At their best, they make us respond to the character, not to themselves.

Actors who are talented enough to submerge their own personalities into the characters they play, and let us believe they are those characters, add immensely to the power of a film. Even the occasional screen icon may do that. Tom Cruise has stretched himself far beyond what he might be expected to do, with films like *Born on the Fourth of July* and *Rain Man* and *Magnolia.* Even Schwarzenegger did it with *Twins.* The point is that without human beings in the film, all that's left is a cartoon.

Part 2 — The Writing

Next, see if the film put your characters into a series of situations in which they had to confront something, learn something, change something, or change themselves. This is the writer's part. The writer thought up the scenes, put the characters there, and wrote out what they would say and what would happen. Did he or she do a good job? Did the scenes seem logical? Was the writer straining to make them work or was it so seamless that you didn't even notice what was happening underneath the dialogue? If you liked what the writer (or writers — in films it's unusual for a film to have just one) did, you can add another plus.

What does a script look like? It contains all the dialogue, often along with the equivalent of stage directions ("Walks to the window, sips from the drink, paces thoughtfully"). It always indicates action, whether or not there's dialogue ("Runs down the alley, shooting at the cop"). It indicates whether it's day or night, whether the scene is interior or exterior, and it also provides descriptions of scenes where no one says anything, such as "Long shot old woman in street, slowly pushing a supermarket cart precariously overloaded with all her belongings, as the rain pounds down on her."

The meat of a film, and its ultimate worth, rests with the writer. A film can be brilliantly acted and wonderfully directed and shot, but without a script it's garbage. Likewise, a great script can be beaten and chopped to death, ineptly acted and poorly directed, but something of the genius that created it will survive. A good critic will spot that and point it out.

Part 3 — The Directing

Ah, the director. Yes, he says "Action" and "Cut." He (or she, obviously) also blocks out where everybody in the scene stands, sits, lies down, runs, drives, flies, kisses, shoots, falls, and dies. The director casts the film (subject to the whims of and any prior agreements between the producer and various agents), rehearses the actors in order to get the most coherent group of performances, and supervises the shooting of every scene. He will often change lines of dialogue during the rehearsal or shooting, replacing what doesn't work with what should work better.

The director is responsible for the look of the film, working with the director of photography (the cinematographer) on how scenes should be lit and shot, and what lens and framing should be used, and whether the camera should be still or move during the shot. The director works with the production designer and art director on the look of the film, and then works with the editor to cut it. What a job, n'est-ce pas? That's why the director gets the big bucks, usually between a fifth and a tenth of what the star is getting. But then again, nobody sees the director.

The director should make sure that everybody connected with the movie is on the same page, figuratively as well as literally. John Singleton's first feature, *Boyz N The Hood* (1991), is a good example of great group work, and he rightfully got credit for handling both cast and his difficult story so seamlessly. But his 1997 film *Rosewood* had a lead actor, Ving Rhames as "Mr. Mann," who seemed to drop in on the production from some other movie, maybe even some other planet. It was as though Clint Eastwood's Man With No Name suddenly appeared in *Sleepless in Seattle*.

Putting it all together

Let's look at two reasonably well-known films — *The English Patient* and *Pulp Fiction* — and see how the three elements work, or don't work, as the case may be. In 1997 *The English Patient* won nine Academy Awards, including the Oscar as best film of 1996, and it was almost universally praised by critics. Much of what we saw on the screen came out of crucial decisions that were made when Saul Zaentz, the producer, and Anthony Minghella, the screenwriter-director, decided to adapt the novel by Michael Ondaatje and cast the leads.

The English Patient

THE WRITING: The novel was long and detailed, with memories triggering flashbacks and a central focus on identifying who the mysterious "English patient" really was. The three parts of the novel were set in World War II England, where the Indian colonial Kim has the dangerous job of defusing German bombs that didn't explode when they landed in London; in prewar North Africa, where we follow the affair between Count Almasy and Katherine; and 1945 Italy, where some of the characters come together in an abandoned monastery just liberated by the Allies. In order to make a conventional-length film (it ended up at 2 hours, 40 minutes) it was felt that there were too many major characters, and too little time to spend with each of them. Moreover, since much of the novel's action took place inside the head of Count Almasy, the "English patient," cuts needed to be made.

If you read the novel and also saw the film you can tell that one early decision was to go with the romantic and sexual attractions between the various characters, and to minimize or eliminate the social and political as-

Ralph Fiennes in *The English Patient.*

pects of the novel. So the affairs between Almasy and Katherine, and Hana and Kim, became the focal points of the film. This was a writing decision.

Did it work? I don't think so. For one thing, unlike the novel, the secret of Almasy's identity turns out to be irrelevant to the outcome of the film, and his actions don't have consequences that affect others. His affair with Katherine, now safely in the past, is literally a dead end. And a relic from the novel, the mysterious thief Caravaggio, who drives what plot there is in the book, is introduced early in the film, forgotten for an hour, then brought back solely to reveal Almasy's identity, by which time nobody cares. In the same way, Hana's brief fling with Kim has no antecedent, because Minghella in his screenplay has left out everything we should know about Kim, the colonial Indian subject who is despised by the British even though he works only to save their lives, at the risk of losing his own. Kim, the most interesting character in the novel, is in the film only to sleep with Hana. So what Minghella gives us is a one-night stand — actually a one-week stand — that again goes nowhere.

THE DIRECTION: Minghella took the three-part story — long, complex, but coherent — and focused on two parts: the Almasy-Katherine affair in Africa in the years leading up to World War II; and the "English patient" lying burned in the old monastery as the war ended. Each of those parts has important emotional components: In each, the characters face death, pain, and violence. But Minghella insisted on directing against the emotions. He held his actors back so there are no outbursts, and hardly even any raised voices, and all pain is intellectual. This can work in a chess match, but in the breadth and sweep of a near-epic story it just undercuts any power the film might have.

Instead, he concentrated on his photography. The desert has never looked so beautiful. The old Cairo hotels are romantic. A church with Renaissance frescoes is stunning. But the movie has no oomph, no zing, and saddest of all no forward motion, no driving force that carries the audience through the story. These driving forces are the responsibility of the director, and here we must say Minghella fails.

THE ACTING: All of the principals in *The English Patient* are experienced actors, well able to create characters and inhabit them appropriately. You might want to question the choice of Ralph Fiennes as Almasy, in spite of his Barrymore-like profile, because as an actor he has none of the magnetism, or charisma, or aura of mystery about him that is the key to Almasy's secret and should be the driving force in the film. But don't blame Fiennes. After all, no actor can do everything, or be all characters; the actor brings only what he or she already has within, and a romantic lead is not within Fiennes's range.

In fact, one of the weaknesses of *The English Patient* has to do in part with the actors not being tested enough. As you watch the film, your sense is that they are all holding back emotionally. Even Kristin Scott Thomas, as Katherine, who has a quite-long deathbed scene, cannot seem to find any way to express herself about it all. Ultimately, in transferring the novel to film, the best and most elusive qualities in the book were lost. Instead of a magnificent epic, *The English Patient* becomes a well-produced soap opera.

Pulp Fiction

At exactly the opposite extreme is Quentin Tarantino's 1994 film *Pulp Fiction*. Not derived from a novel, though it gives a nod of acknowledgment to the 1930s book and film genre that popularized the phrase "pulp fiction" (crime and detective stories that appeared in cheap magazines printed on newsprint, or "pulp" paper, rather than on heavier stock), the film was written and directed by the now-celebrated ex-video-store clerk — just 31 at the time the film was released — with a story contribution by Tarantino's associate Roger Avary.

Pulp Fiction is one of those remarkable creations that despite its title owes little or nothing to any previous film work. It tells us a couple of stories simultaneously. One is about a team of two Los Angeles hit men and their adventures over what appears to be a period of just a few days; the second is the story of an aging, double-crossing, has-been boxer over the same period. They are connected by virtue of the fact that they all work for a crime boss named Marsellus Wallace. At the beginning of the film the hit men and the boxer don't even know each other, but their lives — and those of their boss and his wife — are intertwined so inventively for us that we come to see them as part of a perfectly natural cosmic order. It is the kind of experience in which we take for granted such things as the fact that a character who dies in the middle of the film is still alive at the end; that a particularly comic moment is the question of what to do with the headless body of a man who has just been shot to death, with his brains, blood, and shards of skull smeared all over the inside of a car; that treating the heroin overdose of Marsellus's wife becomes a hilarious experience. People who know the film trade moments with each other as others trade *Monty Python* or *Seinfeld* lines.

But the film is more than moments; there is a complex and carefully worked-out structure that gives weight to the entire movie, enriching the scenes as we watch them, and referring both forward and back to other scenes as well. The film asks us to put aside our notions of the "well-made" film, the traditional structure of a movie that starts, say, with a shooting or a robbery or a deception and then traces the consequences of that act to a conclusion, though it has all of those elements in it. It's not a film about the morality of a hit man's life, or about crime in general, or the boxing world, or the relationship between a crime boss and his underlings, or even about good and evil, though we learn more than we expect to about all of those.

In fact the key to the film is that it doesn't have any overt point of view. There is no right or wrong here. Tarantino is happy to leave all that to others. What he does is set us down in the middle of a group of lives, to watch and listen dispassionately as they experience what you might call some

Samuel L. Jackson, John Travolta, Harvey Keitel survey the damage in *Pulp Fiction.*

very remarkable, life-changing days. And this absence of a governing set of filmmaker's values lends an ironic detachment to the film, a distancing that was incredibly shocking to audiences when they first saw it, and yet has come to open up a whole new way of making movies for filmmakers around the world. No other film since Jean-Luc Godard's *Breathless* in 1959 has had that kind of impact.

THE WRITING: The film begins with a young couple (Tim Roth and Amanda Plummer) at a booth in a coffee shop somewhere in Los Angeles.

They decide to rob the place, but the scene ends as they begin the robbery. We will not see them again until the last scene of the film. Cut to two of Marsellus's hit men, Vincent Vega and Jules Winfield (John Travolta and Samuel L. Jackson) on their way to deal with someone who has tried to double-cross their boss by holding out some unnamed item in a briefcase.[1] The episode will end in a long sequence that has both a multiple murder and an epiphany for Jackson. Next we meet the washed-up boxer Butch (Bruce Willis), who is getting his orders from Marsellus (played by Ving Rhames) to throw his next fight.

Tarantino keeps inventing characters and putting them in intriguing situations, moving them through unexpected developments, as fast as we can assimilate them. Vincent is ordered to take Marsellus's wife Mia (Uma Thurman) out on a date while Marsellus is away. The problem for Vincent is that the last underling who did it was thrown from a fourth-story window afterwards. The date itself is one of the great moments in film, as the two first fence with each other and then go out to Jack Rabbit Slim's, a restaurant where every employee is made up to look like a famous movie or television star.

On and on the movie goes, making bizarre connections at unexpected times and places. Every scene is like another piece of a mosaic, neatly placed so as to enrich our pleasure with the whole. Occasionally Tarantino inserts intertitles ("The Big Fight," though there are no fight shots, and the title appears after the scene's meaning is apparent). At one point Mia describes Vincent as a square, by making the shape in the air; Tarantino gives us an outlined square on the screen as she does it. These aren't authorial or directorial twitches, nor exercises in egomania. Their purpose is to make sure we're keeping ourselves distanced from the action, telling us not to take everything too personally, to sit back instead and enjoy the show. And the show is written so interestingly, with an underlying wit that gives us so many pleasurable shocks — either of surprise or recognition — that we sit for two hours and forty minutes with a kind of silly grin on our face.

THE DIRECTION: This was only Tarantino's second film as director (*Reservoir Dogs* was his first, in 1991), though he had written two other produced

---

[1] Alfred Hitchcock defined an object which appears to motivate the plot, and leads us along through much of the film, but in fact is ultimately seen to be only an irrelevant device as the MacGuffin.

scripts: *True Romance* and *Natural Born Killers*. He took a cast of experienced stars and molded them to a vision that none of them could have expected, because there had never been a film like this before. Early in the film he gives Jackson and Travolta a delicious passage as they head toward a hit on people we haven't met yet. They discuss everything from how you say "Big Mac" in French ("Royale") to what the consequences of giving a foot massage to a woman would be if the woman were your boss's wife. And as they talk Tarantino moves them from driving their car to getting their guns out of the trunk to entering an old L.A. apartment house that seems to have corridors more than a block long. Never a word about what they're there to do, and we're so interested in their conversation that the switch from talk to action seems perfectly normal.

Tarantino fills the movie with bravura directorial moments. When Mia and Vincent are at Jack Rabbit Slim's, the emcee — an Ed Sullivan clone — announces a twist contest. Thurman wants to enter, but — surprise — Travolta doesn't. She has to threaten him with telling her husband that he wouldn't dance. And now Tarantino plays off of Travolta's early triumph in *Saturday Night Fever* twenty years before, the performance that made him a star, where he disco danced to a championship with great flair and power, by now having him barely move his feet at all as they win the contest.

On and on the film goes, never pausing for a conventional moment, never failing to surprise us with new takes on old cliches. Butch the fighter has double-crossed Marsellus by not throwing the fight, betting on himself at great odds, and trying to leave town before Marsellus can get to him. But Tarantino has them meet unexpectedly when Butch runs into him with his car in a crosswalk. Which in turn leads to the famous torture episode in the gun shop with Zed the sheriff's deputy and the Gimp, who is a creature kept in a barred cage inside a trunk, cloaked from head to toe in studded black leather. Tarantino is so sure-handed that nothing is too far-fetched to play out, and everything works logically in the context of the film. We sit comfortably in the palm of his hand as he shows us his magic.

THE ACTING: This is a film in which the actors must play the most bizarre scenes, and deliver the most unexpected dialogue, with complete believability. John Travolta, who'd been a name for almost twenty years but whose steadily declining career was in the tank by 1994, is asked to play a heroin-addicted, slow-thinking hit man whose idea of a worldly vision (he has just returned from living in Amsterdam for three years) is to describe Holland's laws regarding marijuana and hash. It's a role unlike anything he had ever seen before, and he never wavers in character. He stays completely within himself in both voice and body language. Bruce Willis, as Butch the boxer, has to show us both dumb acquiescence and the ability to create a masterful double-cross plan, at the same time. He plays off his movie persona as an action hero, but does it without showing any awareness of life outside this film. He also lives completely within the part. Samuel L. Jackson's role is the pivot around which much of the rest of the film turns. He is a deadly effective killer, who in the middle of the movie, while killing, finds a message from God that changes his life. Try conveying that yourself sometime. It became a performance that Jackson has repeated in a number of films since, though with diminishing impact each time.

The casting is so good throughout that every time we meet someone new we accept them as a part of our (movie) life. Each actor, no matter how small or large the role, has found a center around which to build his or her character, and it shows in the seamlessness of the film. Even though logically, or rather conventionally, nothing here would make sense in the real world, we have been delighted to suspend our disbelief and enjoy the film.

Okay? There you have some critical notes on two movies. You don't have to be a critic to say what I've just said here. Or to say exactly the opposite, of course. You just need to see the movies and think about them, and then find it in yourself to say out loud what you think. It doesn't matter whether you and I agree or disagree. What's important is that we say why we feel the way we do. The best critics working today — Elvis Mitchell, Roger Ebert, Anthony Lane, Terrence Rafferty — all tell us why. They put themselves on the line, so whether we agree with them or not, we at least know what led to their conclusions. Pauline Kael, the legendary critic of *The New Yorker*, was the very best at this, and if you care about films you'll want to have all the collections of her reviews on your own bookshelves.

CHAPTER 2

THE DIFFERENCE BETWEEN ACTING AND ACTING IN FILMS

We all act. We put on one face for our in-laws, another for our co-workers. Is it the real us when we speak passionately to our lover-to-be? We find our very best selves, or certainly what we think of as our best selves, when we hug our children. But how true are those selves, when in fact everyone has an acting repertoire of personas, voices, looks, and mannerisms that we haul out of the file when needed?

And when do we need those skills? When we have to persuade someone, cajole someone, respond to someone, and yes, even intimidate someone. We know when to be nice, when to be nasty, when to be — or seem — open to someone, when to cut them off. We can hurt someone's feelings, we can salve their wounds, we can comfort them, we can abandon them. We act simply in order to get along in the world, to get our way, even just to survive, in our families, in our work, in our lives. Acting is a survival skill; in a sense it is the lubrication that makes relationships easier and life and love worth having.

But unlike the rest of us, professional actors must learn to behave like other people, who may be quite unlike their real selves. Meryl Streep and Sean Penn have each played more than a dozen very different characters in their careers, characters who may have only the most minimal connection with the real Penn and Streep. How do they do it? Without doubt these two are geniuses in their field, equivalent to the rare, great musicians who can perform a wide range of composers and styles with equally compelling authority. Where most musicians are best in one or another repertoire or era, a few — a very few — are at home in nearly all.

So it is with actors. They have developed their skills and talents to feel at home and do well performing in a certain range of parts, and for the most part they are repeatedly cast in those roles, just as most musicians focus on a limited repertoire. These days it's rare for untrained actors to simply walk onto a stage or into a film or television show and make an impact. Most professionals have had rigorous training in their craft. What does that training consist of? Like a pianist's five-finger exercises or a vocalist's scales, it begins with practice in internalizing and then communicating the repertoire of emotions and feelings that, some day, their characters will have to exhibit on stage or television or the movies. There's voice training, so that the actor will be able to call on different modes and manners of speech in order to convey different personalities and emotions. The training includes playing scenes from well-known plays and films, to learn how to be a character unlike one's real self. There is improvisation, where under great pressure the actor must find a character, inhabit it, act it out as that new person, and communicate it all to an audience of fellow actors. There are classes in movement, dance, and singing. There are endless rehearsals and performances of both classics and contemporary theatre pieces, all designed to hone skills and build the actor's range to its optimum extent.

Does it pay off? The actor David Duchovny, who for seven years had played a paranoid FBI agent on *The X-Files,* showed some other acting chops in an otherwise mediocre film called *Return to Me* (2000), when he curled up in a fetal position and cried his heart out, believably, at the loss of his (screen) wife. The very fact that Sean Penn can make us believe in him as a killer on death row, in *Dead Man Walking,* and then successfully play a flaky 1930s musician in *Sweet and Lowdown* is a tribute to perhaps the most extraordinary range of any actor working today.

Acting in films is both easier and harder than acting in theatre. When we see a play, we see the actors as they look in real life. They move, they breathe, they talk, they walk around. They're just like us. We respond to them as real people, because there's nothing between us and them. That's the genius of the theatre. And — what's often forgotten — we see them, live, with our two eyes. They are three-dimensional figures. But in movies, we've interposed a single eye between us and the characters on screen, the camera's eye, an eye that sees only in two dimensions, with only the illusion of depth. This is critical to the way actors look on screen, and how they must act on screen. Everybody's now a two-dimensional figure, and don't think that doesn't make a difference. Even when we add the sound and movement that come with motion pictures, we're still looking at a flat picture on the wall. And because it's hard to predict just how people will look when we put them into that two-dimensional world, almost every actor must do a screen test for every picture he or she tries out for. Only the biggest stars escape, and even they must test if they want to do a picture that's out of their normal range.

Which is why some of us look great in family snapshots or videos, and some of us run to hide. In every family album there's always an Aunt Emily or Cousin Elsa, and we find ourselves saying, "Oh, the picture doesn't do her justice. She was just beautiful." It's not Aunt Emily's fault; the fact is that the camera loves some people and couldn't care less about others. They look flat and uninteresting, no matter whether they're in the center of a fascinating composition, or shot in glorious light, or even, *pace* Aunt Emily, posed erotically. And it doesn't necessarily have anything to do with what they look like in real life, in a three-dimensional world. They don't even have to be beautiful. The camera just makes a kind of decision, and that decision is based solely on how they look in two dimensions.

So who looks interesting in a flat picture on the wall? Here's a short list: Clark Gable, Humphrey Bogart, Marlene Dietrich, Meryl Streep, Cary Grant, John Wayne, Barbara Stanwyck, Marlon Brando, Katharine Hepburn, John Travolta, Vanessa Redgrave, Kevin Spacey, Emma Thompson, Denzel Washington, Gerard Depardieu, Mel Gibson. Beauty isn't the criterion, though of course for most of the movies' history women were objectified, used as icons rather than as people (Anjelica Huston once said that most women's roles in films were written to demonstrate that the heroes were not gay), and our list is of interesting, not just gorgeous or sexy people. Only a few from that early era survived having been cast as sex objects: Stanwyck, Rosalind Russell, Myrna Loy, and Lauren Bacall come to mind. Certainly it's true that today women's parts in films are written for human beings and not male fantasies, but with the exception of Renée Zellweger and Minnie Driver I don't know of a leading actress who isn't drop-dead gorgeous, and I'd guess that Zellweger was cast opposite Tom Cruise in *Jerry Maguire* for exactly the reason that she's not movie-star gorgeous. Which if true is a fascinating thought to chew over. Cruise, who in any of his films could have any woman in the world, chooses in *Jerry Maguire* the woman who brings integrity to his character's life, despite her ordinary looks.

Let's look at a couple of screen idols. John Wayne was an icon for almost forty years, and even though he's been dead since 1979 he remains a public favorite; hardly a week goes by without a film of his, or even a mini-festival, on one or another cable TV channel. How come? The film scholar and historian David Thomson called him "an actor of noble bearing." I think that gets it exactly right. We love to look at people "of noble bearing," and when we add in Wayne's deep and authoritative voice, which was tempered by not being in the least "theatrical" or affected, we have the makings of an icon. Moreover, Wayne had an athlete's grace when he moved. Who else could climb into and out of a saddle with that ease and authority?

What is also interesting about John Wayne is that he was never a sexual figure on screen. There was no sexual tension in his films. He was a doer of deeds, a righter of wrongs. He barely kissed his leading women. He was more a father figure, or an older brother figure, than an adventurer. There wasn't a bit of the adolescent, or even a sexually active male, in him. In *Stagecoach*, the film that made him a star at the age of thirty-two, he finds the ostracized prostitute Claire Trevor and makes an "honest woman" of her by giving her his family ranch while he goes off to serve time for killing the men who murdered his father. A couple of hugs, no kisses, and we know they'll be partners for life. Whether or not they'll have sex is a question that doesn't come up.

Wayne was wise enough never to stray far from that image, and it stood him very well. Even in his last films, as he was dealing with the lung cancer that ultimately killed him, he never let go of the hard, wise, authoritative screen persona. Among his audience, men admired him, even imitated him, without feeling competitive, and women accepted him as a pure, comforting presence.

At the other extreme is Clark Gable, who for ten years was pure sex — even in an era when Hollywood was at its most puritanical. His first year in Hollywood, 1931, he made eleven films and refined his image as a brash, sexy leading man. By 1934, when he starred in *It Happened One Night* and won an Academy Award, he was a sex object for millions of women and a role model for every young man and adolescent boy. Then, two years later, he was the perfect macho-with-a-heart Fletcher Christian in *Mutiny on the Bounty*, as the charismatic first officer, and he capped his career in 1939 as the carpetbagger Rhett Butler in *Gone With the Wind*. Millions rehearsed his famous last line: "Frankly, my dear, I don't give a damn." It was a kind of

Suave Clark Gable as Rhett Butler in *Gone With the Wind*.

sexy *frisson* for women, and a swaggering dream for men who wished they could be like him.

Gable was not a great actor, but he was a great movie icon. He flashed his smile and the camera ate it up. He spoke in a voice that was tough and sexy at the same time, and theatre audiences went mad for him. He never had the physical grace of John Wayne or Cary Grant, but he didn't need it. On screen he was unique in that his image was as both a man's man and a woman's man. In recent years only a few actors, male or female, have approached icon status. Julia Roberts, John Travolta (briefly), Denzel Washington, and Samuel L. Jackson (also briefly) have been in that very small group. Icons have films written for their screen personas, always a dicey prospect that fails more often than it succeeds.

Although Gable made many more films, even up to his death in 1960, his career might as well have ended with *Gone With the Wind*. He aged without gaining maturity on screen, and gradually faded in appeal. By the time of his last film, *The Misfits*, his face sagging and his voice a croaking whisper, he was nothing but a memory. But for ten years he held America in the palm of his hand. He was dazzling, with know-it-all bedroom eyes and a sexy voice that women adored and men imitated. There was an untamed gruffness to him that combined with his pirate's looks to make him irresistible.

Historically, the screen has rewarded icons even more than it has great acting. That's not surprising, since great acting demands great writing, and the percentage of great writers working in films is no larger than it is in any other art form. It's easier for a studio to hire writers for an icon than for a company of actors, so studios are always on the lookout for new icons. A few years ago they found one in a retread sex symbol, now aged by twenty years from his former glory — John Travolta — and they've been feeding him films as fast as he can make them. Studios try out would-be icons for the very good reason that icons are guaranteed to bring in a certain gross for every picture, and in the film business it's the bottom line that counts.

Probably the most unlikely icon of all is Arnold Schwarzenegger. A professional bodybuilder with a heavy Austrian accent would not have sounded like great boxoffice to a producer in the late 70s, but by the early 1990s he was moving out of the trap of being cast as a frightful villain, and made *Terminator 2*, his first film as hero. With good writing that showed off his real and very wicked sense of humor, his films made a lot of money and he became a household word. He's managed his career well, even playing against his looks and reputation in *Twins*. In the 90s, when he reached middle age, he stumbled, choosing vehicles that were badly written and dull, and it will be interesting to see whether he survives as a star past the age of fifty.

Perhaps the single most important difference between film and theatre is that in film the camera itself is the storyteller, while the actors illustrate the story. In the theatre the audience learns about the play from the actors: from what they say or don't say, from the words or silence or movements or actions given to them by the script. The actors tell the story to the audience, which sees and hears it as it was written. In a film, the camera controls everything, because it determines what the audience sees. It can show an eyelash or a continent, a strawberry or a space ship. It can take us anywhere it wants to in a twenty-fourth of a second, which is how fast it can cut from one shot to another. Jean-Luc Godard, the French New Wave director, said that film is "Truth, twenty-four times a second." It isn't necessarily truth, but motion picture cameras and projectors do run at 24 frames per second, except for special effects like slow motion, when the camera runs faster, and stop-motion, which is shot one frame at a time. In any case, no matter what the camera does, the projector has only one speed, and that is 24 frames per second.

Motion pictures can also do much more, of course. They can split the screen, they can superimpose images on top of images, they can change colors, create a montage of images and effects, shoot upside down, and even backwards (check out the delicious Swedish bookshop scene in *Top Secret!*), and morph — wonderful word — one person into another as we watch. Movies can put dinosaurs in the same frame as humans, and they can fly a helicopter into the Channel tunnel. They do things that neither real life nor even fantasy life can duplicate, and that is part of their genius.

What all this means for a feature film is that we in the audience see only what the camera wants us to see. If two people are in a scene, the camera can put them where it wishes — full face toward us, or in profile, or sitting, standing, walking around, looking at each other, looking away, lit for daylight or night, in silhouette, whatever. In the opening shot of *The Godfather* we see only Marlon Brando's hand, but it is the most powerful element in the shot.

Depending on how the director wants to shoot, the camera can tell us who is good and who is bad, who is dominant and who is not, who cares for another person and who does not. The camera can hint to the audience that something bad, or good, is going to happen to the characters in front of us, merely by showing us something on screen that does not quite belong in the scene we're looking at. The camera can glorify the subject or it can demean it, pander to it or insult it, or remain distant and uninvolved, depending on how it shoots, frames, and lights the scene.

Naturally the camera doesn't do all this, or anything, by itself, and in the next chapter we'll discuss the work of the director. But as an instrument of the director's vision, what the camera sees is what the audience sees. No more, no less. It is possible, though maybe not desirable, to shoot an entire film showing nothing but an actor's eyes, say, while those eyes respond to whatever is being said or done offscreen. What *is* done, with some frequency, is that the camera will avert its eye from a scene — whether a murder or a sex scene — by focusing on something else entirely.

Where does this leave the actor? Simplistically you might say that in films the actor shows, but doesn't tell, what's going on. In the theatre, actors project their voices, and may even exaggerate their small gestures, so that people fifty or a hundred feet away will see and hear them. The actors are telling the story, telling the audience what they're doing. In real life people don't speak quite that loudly, or project their voices when in conversation, or move from one place to another simply in order to change a viewer's perspective about what's happening. That's theatre. But in the movies the camera takes care of all that. Microphones will pick up the lightest whisper, the camera will enlarge the smallest visual detail. But most movies still depend on dialogue and interaction between characters, and since the camera brings the audience right into the characters' space, what the actors do on screen is simply live and be, as though this were real life, or, more accurately, as though the movie were a documentary film about their characters' lives.

Actors on screen talk in normal voices, they gesture no more than you or I do, they function as surrogates for the audience. With the exception of being cast as over-the-top villains, or other characters of fantasy, they work very hard at being normal, and when they overdo their parts we in the audience are uneasy and disappointed in the performance. A number of stage actors, some very successful, have been unable to make the transition to film because of that. Laurence Olivier said that it took him years to learn how to act in films, because he couldn't rid himself of his repertoire of stage mannerisms. More than any other performance art form, movies today want their actors, even the stars — especially the stars — to be as much like you and me as possible. Tom Hanks is a star because he looks, talks, and acts like someone we know. Tom Cruise, apart from the fact that he looks like Tom Cruise, maintains his appeal for the same reasons. The screen personas of Geena

Davis, Julia Roberts, Kevin Costner, John Cusack, Susan Sarandon, and Mel Gibson are simply better-looking, brighter, and wittier versions of ourselves. They were our high school class clowns, or ASB presidents, or college theatre actors. We went to school with them, we might even have dated them. It's hard to imagine anyone having dated John Wayne.

There is a second category of screen actor, working in a whole different category of films, in which the actor is required to show just the opposite characteristics from the ones mentioned above. In these films the actor must disappear inside the character he or she plays. So we never see the real Al Pacino, or Robert DeNiro, or Kenneth Branagh, or Emma Thompson, or Jennifer Jason Leigh, or Meryl Streep, or Tommy Lee Jones, or Robert Duvall, or Sean Penn. What we see is the character they create on screen, and in that sense their work is much closer to traditional theatre than it is to contemporary movies. In general their roles are better written than those for stars who simply play themselves, and when we look back at films that hold up best over the years, we find that films with this second type of actor are better represented than those that rely on star appeal. Certainly the first two parts of *The Godfather*, which had nothing but character actors, are much better films because we weren't looking at stars being themselves.

There's a tendency among some critics to demean iconic actors, when comparing them with character actors. I could argue the opposite. I think it was harder to be Cary Grant for forty years and fifty films than to be Al Pacino as twenty different characters in twenty films. Pacino can always return to himself, someone separate from the roles he plays. Grant was born Archie Leach and created the "Cary Grant" persona when he went to Hollywood at the age of thirty. His famous line was "Everybody wants to be Cary Grant. *I* want to be Cary Grant." Well, was he Archie Leach or Cary Grant? The question must have haunted him whenever he met anyone outside a movie set. Did Archie keep poking out at inopportune moments? Could he be himself? And what self would that be? Difficult questions that make for an insecure life.

There used to be a third category of film actor, back in the thirties, forties, and fifties. Mostly male, the group included Sydney Greenstreet, Peter Lorre, Basil Rathbone, S.Z. Sakall, Martha Raye, Thelma Ritter, and Lucille Ball, among others. They were greatly in demand, hustling from set to set and film to film to play the one character destiny and the studio had marked out for them. When we in the audience saw them on the screen we knew exactly what to expect. They were the foils, the cardboard villains, the comic relief, the necessary opposites to set off the hero or heroine. They had their own kind of screen magnetism, and were as predictable as the stars themselves. They all had distinctive voices and impeccable comic timing, and in retrospect we can see that they were as necessary to the success of films in their era as were the stars themselves. Today, those parts just aren't being written, and the whole category is gone. Only Joe Pesci and Danny DeVito, who have built star careers around their character roles, carry on anything like that tradition.

Why the camera loves John Travolta

John Travolta illustrates the way in which what the camera sees is different from what you and I see in real life. Travolta is no longer the sexy young dancer with the hoody look and manner that made him a star in the seventies. He's thicker around the waist, his face is not aging with grace, and he doesn't have a great voice. But when he is on the movie screen, in two dimensions — as opposed to real life, in three dimensions, where he would disappear into the crowd — the camera somehow finds and holds onto his eyes. He doesn't have great eyes, or gorgeous eyes. He has what you might call bedroom eyes, and those eyes give him a magnetism on screen that few other actors possess. And as an extra added attraction, Travolta still has that killer smile left over from the seventies. When he turns it on, the world lights up. Wisely, Travolta has realized that he could use that smile as well for a villain as a hero, and in *Broken Arrow* (1996) and *Face-Off* (1997) he did exactly that.

We see what that look does in his first return film, that is, the first to give him a new character: *Pulp Fiction*. Even though Tarantino chose him for a role as a quiet, drug-addicted hit man who's not terribly bright, and certainly not a very interesting conversationalist, Travolta held his own against Samuel L. Jackson, an actor who can dominate almost any scene he plays in. He did it because we in the audience find ourselves looking at Travolta's eyes, no matter who or what else is on screen. The eyes direct us to the action, tell us what to look at, what to respond to on screen. They exert an almost magnetic attraction on the audience. They are mysterious, hidden, hooded. We can't see into them. They're small and dark, and it's hard to tell quite where they're looking, but they are the most powerful force on the screen.

Travolta's second film back, *Get Shorty*, might almost have been written for him. The repeated line "Look at me. No, no. Look at me." became a mantra. His eyes, and the smile with which he delivered the line, simply hypnotized whomever he spoke it to and commanded their attention. There was no arguing with it. And for the audience it was a command as well. It ordered us as much as it did the other characters, and unlike them we loved it.

The camera loves Travolta, as it loves many other actors, but it doesn't love everybody. It doesn't love Cousin Elsa, and it may not love you or me either. But for the favored few — provided they have talent — it can bring instant stardom. The rest of us will pay to sit in a dark room and watch them work.

(HAPTER 3

DECIDING WHERE THE CAMERA GOES

This is how every shot, in every film, on every stage or location, anywhere in the world, begins:

"Roll sound."

"Rolling."

"Roll camera."

"Speed."

"And................. Action."

A list of what the director does during a day's filming:

•Looks through the camera during rehearsals.

•Talks with the director of photography about how and where to place the camera or make it move during the shot.

•Talks with the director of photography about how to light the shot.

•Works with the actors to rehearse their lines and movements during the shot.

•Works with the actors and the script supervisor on matching their actions to those of the previous shot.

•Talks with the assistant director about scheduling all remaining shots for the day.

•Talks with the designer and art director and prop supervisor about sets, locations, costumes or clothing for each actor, style of decor, or props needed in upcoming scenes.

•Corrects or changes line readings or actors' movements after each take.

•Watches each take on a video monitor, whose camera is attached to the film's camera so it sees what the film will record.

- Listens while the producer points out that the film is in danger of going over budget, and discusses what if anything can be done about it.
- Meets with the film's producer, editor, and director of photography, and sometimes the actors, to look at the footage (called dailies, or rushes) from yesterday's shooting.
- (Sometimes) calls the writer to discuss changes that need to be made in the script.
- Goes home to work on the next day's shots. Decides on camera placement and movements for each shot, sets actors' blocking for each scene, allots a certain amount of time to make each shot tomorrow, realizes that that will require paying overtime, goes over the shot list again to make cuts if possible, grabs a snack out of the fridge, sets the alarm for 5 AM, falls into bed.

Every director, of every film made, follows this daily routine during the shooting of the film, unless the film is scheduled for night shooting, in which case the day starts at about 6 PM and goes till shooting is done, anytime between 2 and 5 AM. What you have no doubt noticed from this is how little time is actually spent on the artistic elements of the film. The race is to get every necessary shot in the can, to get the best possible performances from the actors in the shooting time allowed, to make sure the film will actually cut together without inexplicable holes in the plot or continuity, and to deliver the film on time.

But since film is an art form, and any decent director must be part artist, what happens is that the director will choose a certain number of scenes on which to concentrate. Those scenes, the crucial ones in the director's mind, will take time to work on, and he or she will arrange the shooting schedule to allow for it. There might be extra rehearsals, or an exploration of different ways to shoot the scenes, or simply an allocation of the time needed to enable the actors to reach into themselves and find the powerful emotions that will go into their performances and be communicated to the audience.

This is where the director earns his or her keep. It's what separates the directing hack from the directing artist. It's the difference between *Sleepless in Seattle* (conventional work by director Nora Ephron) and *When Harry Met Sally...* (artistry by Rob Reiner). The lesson here is that Ephron, who wrote both screenplays (*Sleepless* was cowritten with her sister Delia), did not have the director's vision in *Sleepless* that Reiner had in *Harry*. She is a fine writer, and both screenplays were good enough to sustain their somewhat unlikely premises. But one film has lasting resonance, the other gives up everything in a first viewing, and the difference is largely in the direction.

Where to put the camera, and why it makes a difference

We're always most comfortable talking to people who are at eye level with us. Much of life exists at eye level; if one person sits while everyone else stands, there's an imbalance that's hard to overcome. It's an imbalance that adds tension to the moment, and it doesn't matter if the subject is child care or military secrets. That kind of imbalance can be important in films. In the right directorial hands, at the right time, it will add to a scene a tension and an interest that may not even be mentioned in the script. Conventionally, in films, when the camera photographs two people talking, and we in the audience are interested in what they're saying, the camera will usually be at eye level. In television, there's a slight difference. The cameras are usually set at chest level, looking up a bit at the faces of the actors. It's a way of adding a little power to the image of the actor on screen. Television shows, from *E.R.* to *Friends*, keep the camera there because it enhances the impact of the dialogue, and it's the dialogue that's important, not the visual impact of the shot. An odd camera angle might just be confusing.

But if you think about it, where you place the camera can be very important to the meaning of a scene. Picture two people talking. Now place them, in your mind, at the center of a sphere around them.

You can film them from any spot on that sphere. From eye level, from up above them, from below them (you can shoot up through a sidewalk grating). You can shoot so that both people are equally in the shot, or you can shoot over one person's shoulder and focus on the other's face. And, step two of this exercise, you can make the sphere any size you want. You can go a hundred feet away so they're tiny in the frame, or you can bring the sphere in so close that it goes just around their heads and you shoot closeups of their faces.

So not only are there an infinite number of places on a sphere, there are an infinite number of spheres as well. Add to that the availability of dollies, cranes, or tracks from which to shoot the scene, so that the camera can move from one point on one sphere to another point on another sphere during the shot, and the mind can be boggled. And the person who decides where on that sphere, or on the infinite number of places on the infinite number of spheres, to put the camera, is the director.

But we've only started, because next on the menu is the choice of lenses to be used in filming each scene. Zoom lenses can change, even during a shot, from wide angle to closeup, and fixed-focus lenses offer even wider choices, though they can't be switched during the take. So the director must decide how to frame the action or the actors, and which lens will give the best effect. That's why when you see photos of directors during a shoot they all have that cylindrical thing hanging around their necks. It shows them the framing they can get from any particular focal-length lens. And yes, it's heavy.

Did we mention lighting? Not yet. The director and the cinematographer work together on choosing how each scene will be lit. Let's start with television sitcoms. Every set is pre-lit, and every bit of the set is lit to about the same light intensity. There are no bright and dark places. That's because only the dialogue matters, and whether the lines are delivered from the front of the set or the back, from the left or the right or the center, the actors must be equally visible. In films, though, anything goes. Actors can be shown in silhouette or in full front light. One can be visible, another invisible. Cellar steps can be creepy or homey. On location, if a romantic mood is appropriate, the crew will wait for what's called "magic hour," the period just before and just after sunset when film can capture a golden glow or aura around everything.

If it all sounds complicated, it obviously is. But equally obviously we're not talking major angst here. Directors aren't paralyzed by fear of the overwhelming number of possibilities available to them. They work from a film script that creates characters, events, scenes, motivations, and conflicts which all call for more or less logical camera placement and lighting choices. There's a "right" place and a "wrong" place to shoot from, and a "right" and "wrong" way to light, and although a director can violate the conventions at will, it's a good idea to make sure there's a rationale behind doing it. Moreover, many stars want to be seen in closeup wherever possible, and some, notoriously Barbra Streisand, prefer to be shot only head-on or from their "good" side. All these conditions militate against exotic camera placements or bizarre lighting.

Another factor has to do with the style of editing that's common in American studio-produced films. Over the years a convention has become established that dialogue scenes will be made as follows: the actors will play the scene, and a "master" shot, that shows whoever is in the scene and includes all dialogue from beginning to end, will be made. When an acceptable take is approved, then the director will shoot closeups of each individual in the scene. This is done so that the film's editor can cut the scene more quickly and easily. It's the process that's used in television, where editing time is short and deadlines are close. If the director has some clout, and if there's enough time after shooting the master and closeups, the director may then choose to shoot the scene in a different way, perhaps all in one take, with new camera movement or different lighting, in order to reflect or enhance a point the director feels the film needs to make. The best recent example of this, because it violated almost every convention of editing, is *Pulp Fiction*, where Tarantino never once made a conventional edit.

But the convention is the dominant paradigm, as they say, and it is a far cry from the view that's common among film scholars that the director is the auteur, or author, of the film. In the silent era, a few directors had carte blanche to make films any way they wished. In America, that meant D.W. Griffith, Charlie Chaplin, and Buster Keaton. Chaplin particularly was notorious for the time he took to make his films. *The Gold Rush* took a year and a half, and *City Lights*, which he started in 1928 as a silent film, wasn't finished for another three years. But Chaplin owned the studio. At the same time Erich von Stroheim, who as a German directing star had been brought over from Europe to make films here, had his 8-hour epic *Greed* cut by the studio to just over two hours.

As the studios' power grew stronger, directors were put on shorter and shorter leashes. Through the 1930s and 40s they were contracted to particular studios, had little say in what films they shot, and often didn't even see the scripts or meet the actors till a day or two before shooting. Things had loosened up a bit by the 50s, when studios began making wide-screen epics as a way to hold onto audiences they were losing to television, because bigger budgets meant more wiggle room for the directors. And at the same time the Directors Guild of America began asserting its negotiating power against the studios, gaining a measure of independence and flexibility for its members.

The New Wave and the "Auteur" theory

And then, in the late 1950s, a group of young French film enthusiasts, most of whom had been critics for film magazines, began writing and directing their own movies, with small budgets, often using friends and families to fill out their casts. They supported each other financially, taking turns producing the films and shopping them around to distributors. Their first famous success was Jean-Luc Godard's groundbreaking *Breathless* (1959), perhaps the most influential single film stylistically of the sound era. Unlike almost every film ever made up to that time, it was shot largely with a hand-held camera, grabbing shots with available light instead of studio lighting, and making use of jump cuts, in which conventional continuity (successive shots in which, say, the person leaves the house, gets into car, drives to destination, parks, enters another house) is compressed into two shots: person leaves house, cut to person entering the next house. Godard knew somehow that we in the audience didn't need to see every step along the way. We didn't need dissolves or fadeouts from one scene to the next; we didn't even need the action in one shot to match the action in the previous shot.

And then Godard made what would become an even more influential decision: he decided to cut *within* the shot. That is, he would roll the camera during a scene, focusing on someone talking. The shot might last, say, one minute. Then, in the editing, he would cut out sections of that shot, in effect jumping from moment to moment as the audience watches that person speak. It gave an enormous kinetic push to his shots, so that instead of relying solely on what the subject was saying to make a point, the audience would get two perspectives at once — that of the subject, and that of the filmmaker. It is a technique that simply blasted all film conventions away, and it has been influential not only in how films are edited but in how they are written as well. Parenthetically, Woody Allen's 1997 film *Deconstructing Harry* used that technique, but misunderstood its purpose and ended by simply giving the audience snapshots of static scenes instead of adding a forward thrust.

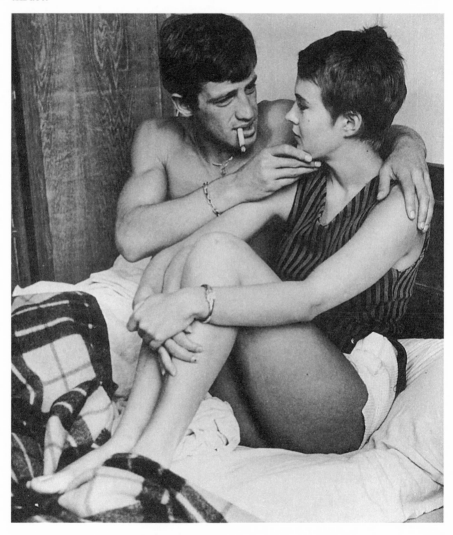

Jean-Paul Belmondo and Jean Seberg in *Breathless*.

Godard's story was about a young American woman in Paris (Jean Seberg) who sells the *International Herald Tribune* on the street, and whose boyfriend (Jean-Paul Belmondo) is a murderer on the run from the police. The pacing was fast, the dialogue elliptical. No dissolves, no fadeouts, just cut, cut, cut. Godard called *Breathless* his homage to Monogram Pictures, the quintessential American B-movie studio, though surely more for its themes than its style, because Monogram was never known for stylistic innovation.

A few months later, François Truffaut, who had produced and worked on the script of *Breathless* for Godard, made *The 400 Blows*, an autobiographical story of a young boy who is sent to a reform school. With *Breathless* and *The 400 Blows*, and a number of films from Godard and Truffaut's young colleagues, the group took the film world by storm, and a French critic labeled their films "New Wave." In fact no film, no television commercial, no music video, no documentary made anywhere in the world since then is without evidence of New Wave influence. None. Whenever you see a film or commercial with jump cuts, overlapping dialogue, hand-held shots, and a documentary look — including the deliberate use of black and white film when color is available — you're looking at what you might call neo-new wave.

Although every film director, writer, and actor in the business was entranced with the new style of filmmaking, it took a New York critic to give it a name. Andrew Sarris, who was writing film reviews for *The Village Voice*, pointed out that each of these young filmmakers was at once the creator, writer, and director of his films (the early group was all male), and since they were French he called them auteurs, or authors, of their work. Forgotten for the moment was the fact that up in Sweden Ingmar Bergman had been doing just that for more than ten years with his own films, but Sarris was quick to add Bergman to his pantheon.

The concept of the director as author of his or her films was of course flattering to anybody who made movies, wanted to make them, or even thought about wanting to make them. It was a concept thousands of would-be filmmakers around the world had waited for. And while most of those thousands were quickly weeded out, a few remarkable young filmmakers in the sixties and seventies did survive the inevitable cuts and compromises. In the United States Francis Ford Coppola, Martin Scorsese, Stanley Kubrick, Robert Altman and a few others, found ways to make their own films without studio control. In Italy Bernardo Bertolucci, in Germany Rainer Werner

Fassbinder, in Japan a whole group flourished, as studio production heads around the world tried to be trendy and gave new filmmakers opportunities they'd never allowed before.

But the French had a head start, and throughout the sixties most of the best young filmmakers were based in Paris. They found new ways to shoot and edit and make use of their actors, new ways to write scripts that held together on repeated viewings; in fact they defined whole new concepts of what a one-and-a-half or two-hour movie could be to an audience. In *Jules and Jim,* Truffaut found ways to communicate the changing pace, even the fever, of a three-cornered love affair. The film is set over thirty years, starting in the decade before World War I, and early on Truffaut uses multiple images of the three principals, images that catch the youthful, almost childish, breathtaking heat that they generate in the wild, dissolute time before the war. Then, when the war comes, Truffaut intermixes battle scenes with shots of the bucolic life being led by one couple. After the war, as the unresolved

Jeanne Moreau, Henri Serre, Oskar Werner in *Jules and Jim.*

tensions begin breaking each relationship apart, he works with longer, thoughtful shots that give the audience time to reflect on what the possible outcomes might be. And we are caught up in this triangle of love knowing it cannot end happily but determined also that it cannot die. It is his control of the shots that catches the changing relationships among them and the changing times they live in.

Truffaut's jump cuts and montages were analogous to the emotions of the moment. In youth, the three were reckless and daring. As they grew into a sadder middle age the film seemed to draw breath more slowly, deepening the meaning of each encounter until the startling, shattering, but entirely appropriate end. Truffaut contrasted a musical score that was the essence of romantic escapism with an offscreen narrator whose coolness and detachment added a distance that set everything in a proper perspective. It was an amazing accomplishment for a 29-year-old making only his third feature.

Throughout the sixties films came out of Paris by the truckload. By 1967 Godard had made almost twenty films, most of them unlike anything that had been seen before, including for example *Weekend* (1967), which starts out as a story about an upscale suburban couple who leave for a weekend visit to the wife's mother, and ends 100 minutes later with the death of Western civilization. He manages to put everyone from Robespierre to Alice in Wonderland to a couple of black African garbage collectors into the movie, and still it all makes a kind of crazy sense. Godard and his colleagues led the film world into an era when genius was honored, even at the expense of logic. If you were a director, particularly one who could claim to be an auteur, this was your golden age.

As with all movements, the New Wave aged and mellowed as its members grew older, changed their styles and interests, and in some cases burned out. But the lasting impact of the group on filmmakers around the world was the recognition that there no longer had to be any boundaries in creating and making a movie. Movies were freed from having to be "well made" or conventionally structured, because whatever their subject, whatever their format, whatever their cast or location or dialogue, no matter how far they departed from traditional filmmaking, they were to be judged on their own terms. For the best and most inventive filmmakers, many of whom had felt confined by convention, this lifted a great creative weight and encouraged experimentation. In America, in 1970, Robert Altman took a lovely but conventional comic script about a medical station during the Korean War, and by virtue of overlapping dialogue, quick cuts, simultaneous foreground and background action, and the help of brilliant comic performances from Donald Sutherland and Elliott Gould, made *M*A*S*H* into the emblematic film of the era. That film not only spawned the famous television series, but we saw its stylistic influence — deadpan punchlines, throwaway moments — in every episode of *Seinfeld*, almost thirty years later.

And now a new generation of film auteurs has come along, making films about everything from Gen X angst to age and death, to the mechanics of running an unsuccessful Italian restaurant. They're often ad-hoc coalitions of actors, writers, and directors who work as a group. And they're not necessarily young; many are in their thirties and forties, and have been in and around the fringes of the business for years, but they are just now getting recognition. Not only in America, they're making films in countries from Iran to Ecuador, from Norway to Botswana. And thanks to venues like the Sundance, Toronto, and Seattle Film Festivals, and MOMA's New Directors New Films series, their work is getting shown and seen, and sometimes even bought for distribution. The godfather of this next wave, the one who legitimized the current freedom to create and shoot in the most idiosyncratic ways imaginable, is undoubtedly Quentin Tarantino, the one-time video-store clerk who in 1994 made *Pulp Fiction* and once more turned filmmaking on its head.

Pulp Fiction is deservedly the most famous picture of the nineties, a film so bold that conventional minds were appalled by it. As was pointed out earlier, this is a film that makes us giggle helplessly at the problem facing two hit men when they've spattered their car with the brains and blood of an unintended victim; that makes us laugh out loud at the attempt to resuscitate someone dying of a heroin overdose; that plays off our expectations of seeing John Travolta do the twist and then fools us by having him simply shuffle in place; a film that takes a sly look at *The Godfather* by having its crime boss hit by a car as he carries Chinese takeout over to a house he's staking out; that dares to give us a briefcase with a pulsing glow inside, which we never get to see into, as the film's MacGuffin.

As with artists in any field, filmmakers devour each others' work like starving children in a Dickensian orphanage. When they see something that's new or unexpected, a reach beyond what's been done before, it excites them, turns them on to go further than they had thought possible, drives them to do more and better work, and forces them to rethink their own approach to making movies. There's a cross-pollination of ideas and styles, a ferment of new thoughts and creative work, that leads to better and more inventive films (not always the same thing, of course). And it's not an even-paced, ongoing process. Years, even decades, go along without any new visions, until someone makes a breakthrough. It could be Godard in 1959, or Tarantino in 1994, or Tom Tykwer, with *Run Lola Run* in 1999, but when it happens it blows the film world apart, and it can be years before the dust settles. In evolutionary theory it's called punctuated equilibrium, and in film it doesn't have a name, but the effect is the same. Films are still made of the same materials: chemical layers on acetate, going through a machined camera at 24 frames per second, developed in the lab and projected on a screen; but they'll never look quite the same again.

Why your films look different from Ingmar Bergman's

We all grow up with photographic images. They're the shots of our family members, standing at the front door, or at a picnic, or on the porch, or the annual Christmas gathering. We took those shots because we wanted to memorialize the moment, so we could always have the memory of Uncle Jack, Cousin Vera, Dad, and our sisters, brothers, and ourselves as we were at that moment. The pictures were taken from the front, in sunlight or with a flash. Everybody looked at the camera and was told to smile. For some families, many years ago, there was an 8mm or even a 16mm movie camera to take pictures of the children. They were told to walk toward the camera, or wave, or run, or hug, or dive into the pond. It was an art form limited by the conventions of middle American life. With the introduction of the camcorder, amateurs got a bit bolder, which led to the popularity of *America's Funniest Home Videos*.

For most of us, that's as much as we want to do with film or video. But for the few who are destined to become film artists, having a camera or camcorder, or even a brain that functioned as one, as a child, was the key to the candy store. Ingmar Bergman made up elaborate stories, put together puppet theatres, used "magic lantern" projection devices before movies even came to his town. Those images and stories, built out of a need to fantasize a world he could be comfortable in, became the source of the films he later made. He didn't know the "right" way to do things, so he never bothered to unlearn any "bad" habits. If the stories worked for his puppets, they would work when humans acted them out. As a filmmaker he wrote his own scripts and had an astonishing eye for good composition within the frame. He chose actors with compelling faces, and his women were stunning (like George Balanchine with his ballerinas, he married most of his leading actresses), and all were superb at conveying what he wanted the audience to learn from the films. He was not afraid to violate any convention that stood in his way. There is a famous scene in *Persona* in which a woman tells another of an erotic encounter she had on a beach, years before, with a girlfriend and two young men. The scene is done in one eight-minute take, as the light outside gradually fades to night and the room gets darker, and the story gets sexier, until the screen goes black and we can't even see the women; they're barely silhouettes. And by the end of the scene the theatre audience finds that it's been holding its collective breath all the time.

It is this kind of boldness and absolute certainty that what is shot is exactly right that separates the film artist from the rest of us. And if time validates the artist's choices, and the film continues to move or excite or

Bibi Andersson, Liv Ullmann comparing faces in *Persona*.

satisfy us, then we acknowledge the work as having greatness in it. As with music or paintings or novels or poetry, we find that we need films in our lives, and ultimately we move from specific films to the filmmakers themselves. We find ourselves asking what makes so-and-so's work different from some-one else's, and we make value judgments about them. Ingmar Bergman could no more have made *Jules and Jim* than he could have flown to the moon. But only he could have made *The Seventh Seal*, and we are all the better for it.

CHAPTER 4

THE ESSENCE OF STYLE

"It don't mean a thing if it ain't got that certain je ne sais quoi," is the Peter Schickele version of Duke Ellington's famous line, "It don't mean a thing if it ain't got that swing." That swing, that "I don't know what," is the signature of the artist. Ella Fitzgerald could sing the same songs as Sarah Vaughan, but you'd never mistake one performer for the other. Cezanne and Monet painted some of the same landscapes, Faulkner and Hemingway both wrote hunting stories, Chaplin and Keaton used some of the same gags. Would you confuse them? Of course not. The old song said, "It ain't what you do, it's the way how you do it." If you and I were given the same film script and asked to direct it, even with the same cast and crew, we would make two very different films. We're different people, we see many of the same things differently, we put our emphasis in different places. You might shoot a lot of closeups because you want to communicate the power of certain relationships or the individual reactions of the characters. Martin Scorsese is known for doing that. I might shoot from a distance because I see a certain irony in what the characters are doing. Quentin Tarantino often puts some distance between the characters and the camera.

There's no right or wrong to style or sensibility, but if you're going to make a decent film you have to have them both, and the best films show them. You can't just put a thousand shots together along a plot line and expect to come out with a movie that people will want to see. You have to have something that swings, something — Schickele's "I don't know what" element — to take your film into territory that's emotionally powerful, or exciting, or witty, or memorable. Style. And substance, of course. Something that makes the film worth seeing. Some filmmakers have it, and some don't. This chapter is about how to tell whether a filmmaker has it, and if so, what it is.

First, let's remember that style, in the sense of an artist's recognizable and unique approach to the creation and structure of a work, is a fairly recent construct. Until the late nineteenth century, most artists — composers, painters, sculptors, novelists, playwrights, poets — worked within the contexts of the genres and traditions that were dominant at the time they lived. Certainly the great ones stretched the limits, and even anticipated future movements in their art forms, but their work was still recognizable as the product of a long tradition. Revolutionaries were few and far between.

But film is a twentieth-century art form. It had no antecedents, and it wasn't a natural outgrowth of another art. It came with no history, no tradition, no "right" way to do things. To the extent that it photographed actors in a story, it couldn't duplicate the stage because it had no voice; for the first thirty years, no one spoke in the movies. Film used photographic emulsions to make the images on each frame, but each frame was different from the one before and the one after, and they all were projected on a screen in sequence, so it wasn't like still photography or painting. So when motion pictures were invented, everyone with a camera was free to start at a point of his or her own choosing. There wasn't a right or wrong to anything. Of the first filmmakers, the Lumière brothers made documentaries; they're known for their famous shot of a train pulling into the Gare St.-Lazare — a shot made from the end of the track, so the train comes directly toward the camera. It was so startling and frightening that people leaped to get out of the way of the movie screen. Simultaneously, the other great contemporary of the Lumières, Georges Méliès, filmed fantasies on a stage about rocket flights to the moon.

So for the first time an art form was born without parents — an almost immaculate conception. There were no rules, there wasn't even a tradition, and style could be as important as substance. Though dramas were produced, the fact that film reels were no longer than 10 minutes made it easier to do comedy. Slapstick ruled and audiences had their favorites. People might prefer the slapstick of Chaplin, say, to that of Mack Sennett's Keystone Kops, even though the gags were often identical. It's easy today to look back and say that it had to do with one being a genius and the other a skilled craftsman, but at the time each was equally popular. A better dichotomy would be between Chaplin and Buster Keaton, who represented polar opposites in silent comedies. Who was better? To this day they each have their partisans. The important point is that each of them was able to project his own vision as an artist in the medium, and each of them was instantly recognizable.

Is this true today? Without looking at the credits of a film, or reading about it, or hearing someone discuss it, is there some way we can tell who made which movie? It's not so easy. For the most part, particularly since the advent of sound, it's been the studios that have decided who worked and who didn't, and whose vision would appear on screen. A lot of movies are like a lot of novels, which are written (or edited) to a formula. They're designed to make money, rather to than express an artistic vision, and in an art form that can only diminish their value. They're designed to fit a certain audience niche. Titillating comedy, say, 12-to-19-year-old girls. Monster adventure, 10-to-17-year-old boys. Serial killer on the loose, 16-to-25-year-olds of both genders. Middle-aged romance, 40+ couples (and not too many of them).

It isn't news that movies are a business. Every year American studios produce enough prints of enough movies so that if all of them were unspooled from their projection-booth platters they could tie the earth to the sun with a bow big enough to float Venus through. Double that if you add in the rest of the world's production. And every year most of those films sink into video purgatory without a trace. Why? An easy and not inaccurate answer is that they just aren't worth remembering. They take up ninety or a hundred minutes or so of the time people pay to sit and watch them, and then those people get up, leave the theatre, and go on with their lives. If the films are remembered at all, it will probably be for a moment or a line or a joke. Every week studios and banks bet millions of dollars that they'll make a profit, and thousands (many thousands) of people work in what is rightly called the "film industry."

In the same way that bad money drives out good, so bad films can clog up the lines from creation to production to distribution to exhibition of good films. Good films are honored less for being good than they are for making money, and good film artists find it harder to get financing than those who make formula films. But having said all that, the fact remains that good films stay alive longer, and ultimately return decent profits to the studios, because — well, because the word gets around that the film is worth seeing. They're like the backlist of a good publisher. Sooner or later the work will find its audience and the publisher — or the studio — will start seeing the money. The question for the studio is how to tell who's good and who's not. But studios are notorious for not trusting their own judgments or intuitions. They'll screen and screen and screen, before different audiences, to judge the demographic appeal of a film. They'll try new endings, new openings, new plot lines. They'll discover that the second lead has more appeal than the star, and — if they can do it contractually — they'll change the whole emphasis of the film. They'll edit sex in or out, depending on the MPAA (Motion Picture Association of America) rating they want to get. Films aren't films; they're product. There's less of a difference between a Hollywood studio and Tyson's chicken farms than you might suspect. It sometimes seems that films worth seeing — works of good film art — get their financing and distribution more by accident than anything else. If it weren't for the insatiable drive that goes with being a good artist, many more filmmakers would now be back working in the family dry-cleaning business.

So what identifies a filmmaker? What makes his or her film worth seeing? Worth remembering? Worth seeing twice? Worth enjoying in retrospect as much as — or more than — you did the first time you saw it? Let's go back to the auteur theory for a minute. The auteur theory said that the film's director is the actual author of the movie. That by making casting decisions, by choosing how and where to put the camera, choosing how and where to put the actors in each scene, how and where to place the lights, and how and where to edit the shots in post-production, the director becomes the film's author. More than that, at the time auteurism was most in vogue, back in the sixties and seventies, many of the world's best directors were also the writers of their films. Few of them were American, because the American studio system separated writers from directors and directors from actors. In Europe and Japan, though, directors either wrote their own scripts or worked closely with longtime screenwriting collaborators. Luis Bunuel, an auteur to his fingertips, worked with screenwriter Jean-Claude Carrière on the four final masterpieces that capped his career, from *Belle de Jour* to *That Obscure Object of Desire*. Carrière, thirty years younger and just starting his own career, somehow found a way to give Bunuel the kind of sensual, magic realism that he was looking for.

Auteurs also had whole repertory companies of actors whom they used over and over again, in film after film, as they did with their cinematographers and editors. Bergman, Fassbinder, Fellini, Godard, and Kurosawa come to mind. This was not possible in the United States, because all parties normally made their own separate plans and schedules. Actors, for example, might be committed to a studio for three films over a two-year period, but the studio would get to choose the films and directors. Similarly, directors had to pick up work wherever they could, even if it meant putting their own projects on hold. Screenwriters were out of the loop in any case, offering their work to whomever would option it.

What does an auteur's work look like? Recognizing it isn't as simple as, say, identifying the unique brush strokes of Van Gogh, or examining Chuck Close's assemblage of tiny doughnuts and hot dogs that he's placed in a thousand grid spaces on the canvas so that they add up to enormous photo-like portraits. No one imitates those. But in film, which imposes many conventions on its artists, we can still find distinguishing marks. Alfred Hitchcock raised melodrama about as high as it can get without falling of its own weight. He himself said to Peter Bogdanovich in a famous interview that melodrama was built backwards. One made the story and then added the characters. That insight is doubly revealing, for drama — Ingmar Bergman's kind — requires first that we know and care about the people who inhabit the films before we care about the plot of the film.

We know that Hitchcock had a style, but how do we define it? With few exceptions his suspense films begin with an innocent or unknowing man (rarely a woman), an ordinary person, who is deliberately sucked into a plot he knows nothing about, by criminals or spies. And Hitchcock makes sure that we identify with the innocent person. Of course that in itself isn't enough to define his work. But then he adds location. In film after film, we see that the initial contact between the innocent protagonist and the bad guys — the event, the crime, the mistake — takes place in a public space, in the middle of a crowd or event, on a train or at a concert or in an open market. The protagonist is leading his normal, unaware life, and then he's forced to run to save himself. Why doesn't he go to the police? Because Hitchcock has devised a plot line that has the police mistake the hero for the villain. The hero can't go to the police. He sets it up as a race against time and death. And then there is an interesting stylistic sidelight for Hitchcock. For the denouement, the revelation of the crime, the clearing of the name, the bringing to justice of the criminals, the re-establishing of order, he will make more intimate shots, in one-on-one setups, as a cathartic restoration of the proper world. It is a structure, a formula, that Hitchcock came to early in his career, and it served him very well for many years.

Quentin Tarantino, whose body of work as of this writing is still small, has already established an identifiable approach. His camera is an extension of the audience. It is our view of events and people. As the camera moves through his stories, it takes our place. It observes, it stands back and watches, it comes in close if needed, then steps back again. In his brilliant *Jackie Brown* (1997), he brings us closer to his people than he had previously, so that we care about what happens to his heroine Pam Grier and her friend Robert Forster. But still, his camera is a kind of onlooker, perhaps standing with folded arms checking out the scene in front of it. In a sense he harks back to the nineteenth-century novel, where the novelist was transparent, was simply the storyteller, without imposing an author's personality on the story. Not that Tarantino is naive. There is a sophistication, an irony, a sensibility that reminds us of Thackeray's *Vanity Fair*, that permeates every story he tells, and it is part of his genius that we in the audience get it. Someone once said that irony is what doesn't play outside New York, but Tarantino's work is powerful enough that he has already become the greatest stylistic influence on films in forty years. Both Hitchcock's and Tarantino's crime films have wit and a sly view of the people in them, but you'd never mistake one for the other.

Probably the very best example of the director as auteur is Ingmar Bergman. You need only watch a minute or two of any of his more than forty films to know that no one but Bergman could have made them. How do you know? Because everything you see and hear, in every frame of every shot, reflects a style, a sensibility, that's as individual and recognizable as Charlie Chaplin's. Bergman's plots deal with serious, life-altering issues that can make or destroy a marriage or a family. His scripts give the actors lines that are intense, confronting, and insightful. There isn't a joke or a moment of irony anywhere, and the body language of his actors reinforces it. That's one element of his work. Then, if we look at his shots, we notice that he's rarely concerned with location, with landscape, or with, say, the beauty of the countryside, unless they illuminate some aspect of his characters' relationships. The camera is in the actors' faces, rarely staying very far back from the action. There is little else to look at in his scenes except the actors.

Bergman wrote most of his own scripts (he was an enviably fast writer; some of his great films were written in two or three weeks), and although he's rightly honored for his direction, the materials were all there in the actors' lines. His scripts were never shy about confronting even the most painful elements of life and personality; in a sense they reveled in exposing intimate secrets and shameful acts. Yet there was nothing pornographic about his work. His characters confronted cowardice and guilt, and lives lived without virtue or meaning, rather than simply illicit acts.

And for more than forty years he had an amazing group of actors, who somehow managed to find it in themselves to illuminate every nuance of those scripts. They seemed to have the ability to let us see into their very souls. Their talent was to find the most vulnerable spots in each of us, the audience, so that we too would open ourselves to the pain. No other film artist I know has ever created a body of work so deep, so revealing, so able to penetrate our innermost beings. The only comparison I can make is with the great choreographer George Balanchine, whose works were illuminated over many years by a seemingly inexhaustible series of premiere dancers who somehow had the ability to reveal the essence of life, emotion, and thought, in ballets so abstract they didn't even bother with a story line. Bergman's acting company, who as they aged and matured moved slowly through his films to play different roles — most notably Liv Ullmann, Bibi Andersson, Max Von Sydow, and Gunnar Bjornstrand — were like Balanchine's succession of principal dancers, who communicated the power of his work for more than forty years.

Naturally, the equation of style with quality has an exception, and the exception is Howard Hawks. In a fifty-year career, from 1920 to 1970, Hawks made more wonderful films, certainly more worthwhile films, than anyone else working in America, and I would defy you to identify his style. The films include *The Dawn Patrol* (adventure — 1930), *Scarface* (crime — 1932), *Twentieth Century* (farce — 1934), *Bringing Up Baby* (romance — 1938), *Only Angels Have Wings* (adventure — 1939), *His Girl Friday* (screwball comedy — 1940), *To Have and Have Not* (romance/adventure — 1944), *The Big Sleep* (crime — 1946), *Red River* (western — 1948), *Rio Bravo* (western — 1958), and at least a dozen more that are on various best-ever lists. Hawks could direct every one of those genres equally well. He insisted that he never tried to impose his own style on a story, but looked only to bring out what was already there. However, Hawks had a most massive ego, and never a moment of self-doubt. He relied on his intuition and trusted it completely. His directions to the actors were along the lines of "Just keep talking and nodding your head," and "Don't get carried away and cry; just say the lines." Wit and action replaced insight and depth, but somehow it almost always worked, and although there never was a Hawks "look" or "style," there will always be Hawks films.

But in spite of Hawks, style in the largest sense won't just go away. It's how we think about what an artist means, and it's part of what makes him or her different, better, or worse than someone else. Elizabethan scholars point out that the essence of Shakespeare's genius lies not in his plots, not in the action of the plays, and not even in the scenes and situations, but in his poetry, his language, his ability to reveal his characters in the lines he gave them. The value of Shakespeare is that we can see ourselves in his people, and come to understand our lives more deeply than we would have without him. Film at its most valuable can do the same thing. Much of its power, certainly, lies in the lines the characters speak, but much also comes from where the filmmaker stands in relation to the characters. How they are shot and lit, and how the film is cut, become powerful tools for the film artist. If the filmmaker controls them, then camera placement, lighting, and editing, and even the choice of music and sounds behind the action, contribute to the worth of the film as art.

Many film textbooks talk about lighting. Stand someone in front of the camera, and light them from the front, and they may look flat or uninteresting. Light them from the side and there is a more intriguing, or perhaps sexy, quality to them. Light them from behind, so they are in silhouette, and they acquire mystery. Light them from above and they are either saintly or evil. All of these can work where they're appropriate. But the best filmmakers know how to combine them with motion. Instead of a still shot, picture a young couple, in danger but unaware of it, walking down a sidewalk, with the late afternoon sun casting their long shadows before them. The camera is shooting from behind and a little to the side, and it tracks along with them. So we see the couple and their shadows, and we hear the click of their heels as they walk. The camera moves in and tilts down so it's concentrating just on the two shadows. But then we see the shadow of a third person, slowly gaining on them. First the shadow of the head, then the body, as it gets closer, still behind them but slowly closing in. Add in music or sounds that reflect the ominous approach of the unknown person casting the shadow, and we have suspense. All in one shot. That's the movies.

Everyone who's ever made a film knows that shot; it's a cliche. But everyone who's ever made a film also knows that it still works, that it can still be effective. The question for the filmmaker is to ask whether, if the shot is appropriate, it should be used, or some other device should be used instead to indicate ominous suspense. How the filmmaker answers the question says a great deal about his or her style. In the 1940s and 50s, a genre of movies called "film noir" had a minor vogue with audiences, and a powerful impact on filmmakers — an impact that has lasted till the present. By the mid-90s, a whole style called neo-noir had come into its own as an important kind of film. Movies like *Red Rock West* (1993), *The Usual Suspects* (1995), and *L.A. Confidential* (1997) are examples of the genre.

Noir films had a dark sensibility — not black, as the word literally means, but rather deeply shadowed instead. They weren't like Hitchcock's crime films, which early on were often bright and funny. They were films like *The Verdict* (1946), *Scarlet Street* (1945), *The Woman in the Window* (1944), *Double Indemnity* (1944), *The Big Sleep* (1946), *The Asphalt Jungle* (1950), and *Kiss of Death* (1947). You might almost say that they were studies in deserved or undeserved death. If they had wit it was black humor; if they had a moral it was hard to find. Were it not for the industry's Production Code, which mandated for all films of the era that good triumph over evil and criminals not be seen to win, the films would have been even more powerful.

Noir films were low-budget productions about crimes and criminals. Because there wasn't money for big sets or A-list casts, the filmmakers concentrated on atmosphere, dialogue, and plot. Lights and shadows stood in for sets and props and locations. Most of them were shot on the studio back lots, and on sound stages using leftover pieces of sets from other films. More than a dozen different directors made them, and yet they all look like siblings. They're examples of what Stephen Jay Gould would call "evolutionary convergence." They weren't related, but they pretty much looked alike, and so style here must describe the group, rather than any individual filmmaker.

Where else do we see an identifiable style? For almost sixty years, from *Snow White* through *The Lion King*, Disney animated films were unique in everything from look and sound to story line and technique. They were called "full animation" because there were no noticeable shortcuts in the animation of every least movement — from rabbits' ears twitching to blades of grass swaying in the wind. When a dinner plate danced with a teacup, it was like a Sotheby's auction catalogue come to life. By the mid 1990s, though, other studios were producing full animation films of their own stories, and technique was no longer a proprietary asset.

"Cinema Purité"

One night in 1995, as the story goes, two Danish filmmakers — Lars Von Trier and Thomas Vinterberg — ended an evening of drinking with what they called a vow of chastity. They swore that they would make films without any, much less all, of the usual feature-film accoutrements: No artificial lighting, no post-dubbed sound or other enhancements, no created music, no studio sets, no special effects, no cinematic shifts in time or space, in fact not much of any of the conventional styles of filmmaking. They refined their vow into a manifesto called "Dogma 95." Each of them, along with a handful of other filmmakers, has since then made films, with greater or lesser success, that mostly adhere to the Dogma rules. They include Von Trier's *Breaking the Waves* (1996), Vinterberg's *The Celebration* (1998), and Von Trier's 2000 festival smash *Dancer in the Dark*, winner of the Palme D'Or at Cannes and the opening night selection for that year's New York Film Festival.

At the same time, some American independent filmmakers who hadn't signed on to Dogma were making films that in their own way broke the conventional barriers as well. *Kids* (1995), written by Harmony Korine and directed by Larry Clark, was a powerful documentary-style look at New York

Franka Potente doing her thing in *Run Lola Run*.

City adolescents living on the edge of death. Darren Aronofsky's *Pi* (1998), shot on high-contrast black and white film and edited like a trip on speed, opened many filmmakers' eyes to other possibilities. The 1999 sleeper *The Blair Witch Project* added evidence that anything that worked could be a winner, and by the summer of 2000, *Premiere* magazine had given all of this a name of its own: "Cinema Purité."

But perhaps the one film that most exemplifies the exhilarating release that this explosion of styles and content has generated — and is in no way a Dogma film — is the German Tom Tykwer's 1999 work of genius *Run Lola Run*. In 80 minutes of screen time Tykwer gives us three versions of a story where Lola must find and deliver to her dumb boyfriend 100,000 marks, or he'll be killed by the gang he's working for. Run Lola, run. Tykwer makes it funny, romantic, and wholly delicious, intercutting everything from ancient sight gags to animation to instant flash-forwards of the future lives of people Lola runs past in the street. There are in-jokes, including an homage to *Pulp Fiction*, but the work is totally Tykwer's own. No doubt others will try to imitate or plagiarize it in coming years, but *Run Lola Run* will stand as the gateway to the new millennium.

CHAPTER 5

WHY WE CRY AT THE MOVIES

The short answer is that we cry at the movies for the same reasons we cry anywhere else: we feel a loss, or we're hurt, or lonely, or sad, or angry, or fearful, or frustrated. If we're emotional we can also cry at the beautiful, the miraculous, the astounding, the unexpected whether good or bad. We cry at the cathartic moment: The birth of a baby signals the arrival of new life from some mysterious hidden place, a new human being that grew, invisible to us, from an anonymous single cell, and then appears at delivery fully formed as a human being — a new creation in the universe. We cry at death; we cry at the imminence of death, at the inexorability of death, at the fear of death. We cry as we grieve. We cry at the triggers of emotion — at the pathetic, sometimes even at the bathetic, knowing that it's insincere but feeling the emotion anyway. We cry at the sacrifice of one life for another. We cry because something has attacked our emotions, overwhelmed our defenses, burrowed inside whatever secret places we keep to ourselves and exposed them to the light.

In one sense art — all art — can be defined as that attacker. And we are the willing victims. We consume novels that reach our emotions; we listen over and over again to music that opens our hearts to bursting. We keep lines, stanzas, whole poems in our memories and recite them almost as a catechism. We don't run from these attacks; we live for them, we search them out, we share them, we're hurt if our friends and lovers don't respond as we do. Throughout history and every culture that ever was, there is one constant: art is what makes life worthwhile, what gives it its primacy in the life of a culture, its resonance in the minds of later cultures. Think of this: For five hundred years prior to the rise of Athens — a period longer than there have been Europeans in North America — the Greeks told each other Homer's story of the Trojan War. They told it because they couldn't read or write. Their education was rudimentary, and they had no context for written language. But they *had* to tell the story; they couldn't let it go, because if they did it would evaporate and disappear; they knew that if ever they stopped telling it, it would be gone forever. What possessed them? Call it the power of art, that insistent, irresistible attack that we seek out from childhood on, a hollow inside ourselves that only art can fill. Children demand to be told stories; give them crayons and they make pictures; when they're alone they sing to themselves, they dance, they tell themselves stories. Making art is as natural to them as eating.

That doesn't go away just because we age into adults. Nothing that powerful can ever leave us, and nothing we do can erase it. But as adults the way we show it is by crying when art affects us. It's universal. Ask anyone what films, what works or moments of art make him or her cry, and you'll get a list that's miles long. My own is enormous, and probably yours is too. Here's a sampler: Rembrandt's late self-portraits, which speak to me as though they were an open-book test of the worth of my life. Sarastro's prayer in *The Magic Flute*. The final duet ("We'll Build Our House") in Bernstein's *Candide*. The chorus of the hymn "On Eagle's Wings." Billy Joel's "Lullaby." Someone more musically knowledgeable than I might find technical similarities in those chord progressions, suspensions and intervals. I simply melt. What else? Debra Winger's farewell to her children in *Terms of Endearment*. I hadn't read the novel when I saw the film, and to this day I cannot pick up the book for fear of facing that scene. As a child the story that moved me to tears was Hans Christian Andersen's "The Little Match Girl," who slowly freezes to death on Christmas Eve as the family inside feasts on a holiday dinner. A 19th century potboiler called *Nobody's Boy* was my novel of choice. My neuroses, of course, and I'm not proud, but you have them too. Art — good art or bad — will do that to you. As a critic I've seen thousands of films, and I still have moments of panic at the thought of revisiting a movie that made me cry; I'm afraid to open old wounds.

Some art is intimate; after all, you don't have to be in the concert hall to respond to music. It's right there on your CD player or radio. But movies are enormous, and are meant to be seen, at least for the first time, on the big screen. They're larger than life, though certainly they are not the first larger-than-life art. After all, the Greeks had theatre festivals and competitions. By the eighteenth century in Europe liturgical music had expanded into opera, which became the larger-than-life art form for two hundred years, with huge voices, choruses, and orchestras filling theatres as emotional stories were conveyed in sumptuous music, reaching the hearts of thousands of listeners with stories of love and loss and betrayal and wickedness and divine retribution, giving us heroes and heroines undergoing agonizing deaths and glorious triumphs.

Since the beginning of the twentieth century, movies have been the whole world's larger-than-life art form. And yet their impact is individual, one-on-one, because movies are about people like us, surrogates for ourselves. They push us into the lives of those people, or perhaps a better view would be that they bring them — those created, fictional people — into our lives. We feel the emotional impact because they're our proxies. A movie that makes us cry has characters — people; human beings — in it who are like us, and their lives have resonance in our own lives. If the things that make us cry in real life come from events in our own lives, then the things in movies that make us cry are the proxies for those events, and the movie characters those things happen to are the proxies, the stand-ins, for us. So why don't we cry when people die in an Arnold Schwarzenegger film, or a *Die Hard*, or a *Lethal Weapon*, or a *Gladiator*? Because the impact of those films is physical, not emotional. They may have wit, they may even have beauty, they certainly have excitement, but no matter how many people die or have bad things happen to them, we don't know or care who they are, we don't identify with them, and we don't cry.

Can we make a list of films that everybody cries at? The perennially popular *It's a Wonderful Life* owes much of its appeal to our response to the injustice done to James Stewart, and the sadness of a life that appears to have been thrown away. Jane Darwell as Ma Joad in John Ford's 1940 film *The Grapes of Wrath*, slowly burning the family photos before leaving for the west, saying goodbye to the past, to all her dashed hopes, to all the years of a life that now seems to have been made pointless and worthless, to have been stomped on by capricious fates that care nothing for one's work, one's love, one's heart, brings my brother Hal to tears every time. When one has suffered a loss — the loss of a child is a parent's worst nightmare — then the proxy for it on screen will bring out every emotion felt in real life. In Steven Spielberg's 1998 film *Saving Private Ryan* we see Mrs. Ryan watch the military car bearing news of the deaths of three sons as it slowly drives up the long dirt road to her farmhouse. Not a word is said, as the camera pans past the "Four-Star Mother" banner in her window. She slowly sinks down onto the porch as she recognizes the meaning of the moment. Whole theatres cry, as they do at the end when, fifty years later, the aging Ryan visits the grave of his captain, the man who died that he might live. Another Spielberg film, *Schindler's List*, provides the catharsis audiences need when we see the survivors pass the tomb of Schindler in Israel, adding stones in memory of the heroism that gave them their lives back.

It isn't always death, but the foreknowledge of dying, that triggers these emotions. Millions of people today, who weren't even alive at the time, cry at Gary Cooper's farewell to the crowd at Yankee Stadium, in the 1942 film *Pride of the Yankees*, as the dying Lou Gehrig says, "This is the greatest day of my life." And this in spite of the fact that Cooper, no athlete, couldn't even pretend to swing a bat with anything resembling major league form. Verisimilitude is irrelevant when emotion is present. The closing shot in the 1943 movie *Bataan* shows Robert Taylor firing an inexhaustible quantity of bullets from the last American-held foxhole in the Philippines as the hated Japanese soldiers come closer and closer. As the camera moves in on him, the words "NOT — The End!" come up on screen. Millions wept.

It's amazing how closely we identify with fictional characters. The first opera I ever saw was *Aida*, at the age of 6. When Radames and Aida were sealed into their tomb on stage — cutaway so we could see them and hear them sing their final duet — to slowly suffocate as punishment, I knew — I *knew* — that those two singers up there on the stage were actually dying before my eyes. It was horrible to watch. One of the first movies I ever saw was *Snow White and the Seven Dwarfs*, and I hid under my seat whenever the wicked witch came on screen; children — even adults, for that matter — don't necessarily distinguish between artifice and reality, nor between animation and live action when the story and characters deal with real emotions. Look at *The Simpsons*. We have great empathy with that family because of their humanity. Part of the power of film as an art form is that movies — images on a flat screen — are so lifelike, have such power to make us feel what the filmmaker wants to convey, that we give up our normal reticence at expressing emotion before others and sit, protected as we think by virtue of being in the dark theatre, with our feelings fully exposed. Were movies shown in daylight we would be much more guarded. And if we see the same film at home, on a television monitor, the image is only a part of the wall, the room, the furniture, the ongoing life around it. Everything it says or shows is diminished. For other than an erotic moment, intimacy is the enemy of impact.

Movies illuminate the fantasies, fears, and insecurities of our lives, the "weaknesses" we can't reveal; they shamelessly pry open our deepest secrets and force us to work through the catharsis of tears. They remind us of our own traumas and tragedies. What are the examples? In *Imitation of Life* a mother is denied by her child. If you're a parent that's one to rip your heart open. In *Saving Private Ryan* Matt Damon tells Tom Hanks, "These are the only brothers I have left," knowing that his own three brothers have already been killed, but deciding to stay with his squad mates and face an overwhelming German attack that's likely to kill them both and make meaningless the whole reason for bringing them together. What is the value to such a sacrifice? It's a question that reaches to the foundation of society. Certainly it brings audiences to tears.

But loss and sadness aren't the only emotional triggers we get from a larger-than-life art form. Comedy — the release of laughter — has an emotional component as well. We laugh as hard as we cry, and there are no conventions of good manners or politesse to keep us in check. No other art form has as many ways to give us the release of laughter. Physical comedy, particularly since the death of vaudeville and burlesque, is now almost exclusively linked to film, though obviously dance has its comic moments as well. See *Singin' in the Rain* for the best example of a film using dance to comic effect.

Are there other emotions that drive the appeal of film? Desire, bliss, and exaltation come to mind. Thousands of films (and also plays, operas, poems, and novels) are romances, works that take audiences along on the roller coaster of love. And we find love in many unexpected places, of course. When was the last time you saw an action film that didn't have a love affair, doomed or otherwise, tacked onto it? Although American studios are blind to many things, they are quite adept at shoehorning a love story into every possible movie, from sports films to war stories, whenever they get the chance, whether appropriate or not, as a deliberate way of enhancing the film's appeal. (The reverse is also true: studios think "pure" romances have too narrow an appeal, and will usually add an element of mystery, suspense, action, or comedy to sweeten the pot.)

But then any work of art — any good work of art — needs to have an emotional component, a perhaps undefinable core that we in the audience can hang onto long after the experience is over. And time has taught us that the best are usually tragedies, works that reach most deeply into us. What makes a tragedy? Its poetry, its humanity, its worthy characters. And then a tragedy must have a catharsis — I should say *only* a tragedy can have a catharsis — a cleansing, that lets us breathe the air of life again, that sets the world back in equilibrium again, but in a different equilibrium, a different stasis, from the one it began with. Movie studios shy away from tragedies, of course, because few of them make back their investment, but ultimately it is tragedy that defines any culture, any era, that makes it worth remembering, revisiting, and learning from. Few filmmakers have the genius to write meaningful tragedies, and many films of tragic plays or novels find their impact diluted on the screen. One reason is that the filmmakers are making a movie and not a tragedy. For example, no totally successful film has yet been made of *King Lear*, but Akira Kurosawa's *Ran* (1985) — which is actually a meditation on *Lear* rather than a production of the play — is in its own right every bit as powerful a tragedy as the Shakespeare play. Does it matter in America that the film is in Japanese and that we sit in the theatre reading subtitles? No matter where we sit the film overwhelms us, and the lesson is that a film artist who dares to attempt a tragedy must do the tragedy itself, take his or her chances, and not simply make a movie and hope for the best. But tragedy or not, almost any film with an emotional component will bring *somebody* in the audience to tears, which is actually a very good thing.

CHAPTER 6

WHAT WE LEARN FROM
BUSTER KEATON

We forget how hard it is to be funny. It takes talent to do drama, but it takes genius to do comedy. Think how many ways one can say a line of dialogue, or pick up a cantaloupe at the supermarket, or kiss a child goodbye, or talk on the phone. Basically, there are as many ways as there are actors to do it, and most of them will work adequately if not perfectly. Now think how many ways there are to tell a joke, or do a pratfall. There's only one way, unless you don't want to be funny. Knowing how to pick that one way, and then telling the joke with proper timing and inflection, or selecting exactly the right way to trip, fall, run, throw the pie, or react to getting hit with the pie, is what takes genius. It's why so few of us are funny, and why we give comedians such a visible place in our lives. There are a thousand actors for every worthwhile comedian.

You could say that in the history of American film there have been three great eras of comedy. The first, of course, was the silents, with Chaplin, Keaton, and their cohorts and competitors all in their prime. The second was the nineteen thirties, with comedies like *Twentieth Century* and *His Girl Friday* and the Marx Brothers films, that depended on verbal wit and repartee rather than plot or character for their success. Then there was a long hiatus until the arrival in the 1970s of Woody Allen's purest comedies: *Sleeper* (1973), *Love and Death* (1976), and *Annie Hall* (1977), followed in 1980 by Zucker, Abraham, and Zucker and their friends, with films like *Airplane!*, *Naked Gun*, *Top Secret!*, and which subsequently, in fits and starts, has lasted till the new millennium through the films of the Coen brothers and the Farrelly brothers. Three eras, three totally different styles.

I add these caveats: First, the 1956 Danny Kaye film *The Court Jester*, appearing out of nowhere at the time, has the two greatest comic sequences since the introduction of sound, and belongs in anyone's pantheon of comedy. Second, Robert Altman's *M*A*S*H*, of 1970, is sui generis for its completely go-to-hell style of direction and comic action, converting the throwaway line into a moment of genius, and breeding every television sitcom for the next thirty years. And third, the Monty Python films of the mid-1970s, which stood traditional comedy on its head by turning absurdity into the everyday currency of life. Nevertheless, the essence of film comedy was defined before 1920, by the geniuses of the silent era.

What makes comedy funny? Let's look at the silents, and remember that silent comedies aren't just for children's parties. Adults weren't so innocent back then that they didn't know what was good and what was not. Chaplin, Keaton, and Laurel and Hardy all knew exactly what they were doing — what made something funny, and what didn't. Intuitively they knew more than the Farrelly brothers and Woody Allen put together. And we should remember that the Farrellys and Allen have had the advantage of having seen and studied all the silent comedies, not vice versa. Think for a

Buster Keaton checking his firepower in *The General*.

moment about actually working in silent comedy. No funny lines, no wise-cracks, no verbal communication, period. You couldn't even use sound effects. Just your own body and mind. I'm not demeaning the current comics. They are truly funny, and they are quite skilled enough to know what works and what doesn't. But just as an exercise, let's compare Jerry Seinfeld's television show, which enjoyed a nine-year run at the top of the ratings, with a Keaton movie:

Seinfeld's show was a comedy of moments. His style consisted of the setup, the line, the reaction shot, the wipe to the next setup. There was wit and charm in almost every scene, and in the best episodes many millions sat for a half hour with a nice grin on their faces as comic moment after comic moment went by.

Keaton's style was the setup, the action, the consequence that leads to the next action, the consequence of *that* that leads to the *next* action. Each one is a step higher, harder, and (usually) scarier. Keaton uses that tension to build just one situation into an extended comic sequence, and then sustains it till he's milked it dry.

This is not some new kind of analysis. In 1947 the critic and novelist James Agee wrote a famous piece in Life magazine about silent comedy. He said, "In the language of screen comedians four of the main grades of laugh are the titter, the yowl, the bellylaugh and the boffo. The titter is just a titter. The yowl is a runaway titter. Anyone who has ever had the pleasure knows all about a bellylaugh. The boffo is the laugh that kills. An ideally good gag, perfectly constructed and played, would bring the victim up this ladder of laughs by cruelly controlled degrees to the top rung, and would then proceed to wobble, shake, wave and brandish the ladder until he groaned for mercy. Then, after the shortest possible time out for recuperation, he would feel the first wicked tickling of the comedian's whip once more and start up a new ladder."

So. Your turn. How far up the line did Seinfeld take us?

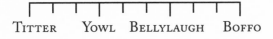

TITTER   YOWL   BELLYLAUGH   BOFFO

My point exactly. Now let's look at one of Buster Keaton's films, *The General* (made in 1926), and I'll walk you through one sequence. The film is set in the Civil War (based on a true incident, by the way), and Keaton is

Johnnie Gray, the Confederate engineer whose proudest possession is his locomotive, named The General. A group of Union spies sneaks through the Confederate lines and steals the locomotive. They head back north, and Keaton sets out in pursuit, alone, commandeering a military train to try and catch them. He notices that behind his engine there's a flatcar with a huge cannon on it, pointed forward and up, at a good angle. He will fire the cannon at the Union train.

There's a big can of powder next to the cannon, and he carefully measures out a small handful and dumps it into the cannon. In goes the enormous cannon ball, he lights the fuse and runs forward to the locomotive cab. The cannon burps, and the cannon ball sails gently up and into his cab. That's step one, the titter. He hurries back, cleans out the barrel of the cannon, dumps in the whole can of powder this time, adds another cannon ball, and lights the fuse.

As he starts to make his way back to the locomotive, the train starts bumping, and little by little the cannon slips slowly down until it points directly at Keaton, with the fuse burning. Step two, the yowl. Now panicked, he hurries across the coupling to the locomotive to hide, but as he does so his foot gets caught, and he is now the one holding the flatcar and the locomotive together, with the cannon about to fire at him. Step three, the bellylaugh. As he extricates his foot and the flatcar comes loose from the locomotive, we see that the tracks now curve left so that Keaton's locomotive moves out of the line of fire and the Union spies' train is directly in line with the cannon, at which point the cannon fires, at the Union train and not at Keaton. The boffo.

Next, we learn how to shoot comedy

Keaton and Charlie Chaplin had diametrically opposed comic styles. Although both had grown up in vaudeville, and both were physical comics, when they got to the movies Chaplin retained his sense of the stage, and for the most part treated the camera as though it were placed in the orchestra of a theatre, just observing the action. He didn't use camera movement or framing to help create his effects. He simply stood the camera up and performed in front of it. The camera might pan to follow him as he moved, but he rarely used tracking shots or cranes. What this means is that his comic sequences are self-contained within each scene. They begin, run their course, and end before the next setup.

There's nothing wrong with that; Chaplin's films are masterful. But when you study them you find that the comic pieces are strung like pearls on a necklace, each one separate from the one before and the one after. His feature-length films were more like three or four of his two-reel shorts spliced together, with only the barest story connecting them.

But Keaton's genius was to find a way to make each comic sequence work first as a part of the film's plot, second to lead us on to the next sequence, and third to still be good enough — funny enough — to stand alone. That's why I say Keaton teaches us how to film comedy, because all three of these characteristics are what we see in *The General*. Let me show you what I mean.

The story is about trains. You can't film a story about trains without putting your camera on the train, next to the train, or inside the train. And if you're next to the train, shooting the film, you need to be moving just as fast as the train itself is moving. In 1926 there were no Steadicams, no helicopters to shoot from, no sophisticated rear projections to put your actors in front of, and definitely no computer-generated sequences. Keaton worked with real trains, on real tracks (in Oregon, near the town of Grants Pass), moving reasonably fast. So in addition to the trains and tracks, he needed a highway or second set of tracks on which to mount his camera and travel along with the trains while he shot some very complicated action. Then he needed to time every action, every comic beat, every visual punchline so the camera would be there in the right place, at the right time, and framed perfectly so the audience would be sure to get the joke. The entire cannon-firing sequence was shot at 30 miles per hour from a moving train on a parallel track that Keaton built about fifty feet away from the action. Think about THAT.

Oh, and one more thing. Keaton, who never went beyond the sketchiest elementary education, had an extraordinary sense of composition. He could frame his shots so that we in the audience see a) only what he wants us to see, and b) everything he wants us to see. Near the end of *The General* there is a battle sequence between the Union and Confederate troops that he has filmed as though it were a documentary of the Civil War. The shots are composed like Mathew Brady photographs, and one shot — of soldiers moving through a wood that's lit by shafts of sunlight coming from behind and half-silhouetting them — was stolen twenty-five years later by John Huston when he made *The Red Badge of Courage*. That shot became the emblematic image of Huston's film, with no credit given to Keaton.

And he had another talent: He had learned that film can create its own magic. In *The Navigator* there's a famous shot where Keaton and his girlfriend are looking for each other and just missing, each running around the deck of a big ship, with one turning a corner as the other comes around. The ship rocks, and all the cabin doors swing open, then slam shut together. There's no sound, of course, but we watch Keaton jump at the noise. Nobody had ever thought of that before. And in *Sherlock Jr.* he went even farther, making his projectionist hero so involved with the story on the theatre's screen that he joins the film as it plays in his movie theatre. If that sounds familiar, better go rent Woody Allen's *The Purple Rose of Cairo*.

One interesting point comes to mind about Chaplin and Keaton. Both made many two-reel shorts before they did their first features. Chaplin's genius seems to have come out best in those two-reelers, which run about fifteen to twenty minutes. His features often equal but don't surpass the shorts. Keaton, on the other hand, made dreadful shorts, and didn't hit his stride until he began making features. I think Chaplin needed the discipline of putting everything into a few minutes of screen time, while Keaton couldn't get anything out until he had the time to work with it.

Now let's come back to television sitcoms for a moment. Sitcoms are shot (with multiple cameras for speed and ease of editing) like Chaplin films. The action takes place on a set, in front of two or three mostly stationary cameras, with people standing, sitting, and at most running into and out of the set. There are pratfalls, but they're all in a confined space. What Keaton did in all of his features was to open comedy out beyond anything that had been done before, and hardly has been done since. Many have tried, and failed, with dreadfully bloated efforts like *Around the World in 80 Days* and *The Great Race*, both of which proved only that it takes a great artist to be funny. As the actor said on his deathbed, "Dying is easy. Comedy is hard."

Certainly films today are verbal more than physical, although in action films there's an ever-increasing competition to do bigger, more bizarre, and more fantasy-driven stunts (witness the leaping, gravity-defying bus in *Speed*). And almost since the coming of sound, comedies have been dependent on language. Not necessarily witty conversation, but the use of language to provide the laughs. Generations of college students have memorized every line in *Monty Python and the Holy Grail* because the unlikely juxtaposition of dialogue, rendered absolutely straight, with the most bizarre visual plot situations, makes each scene a comic wonder. Who can forget the knights who say "Neeh," or the three questions ("What is your name?" "What is your quest?" "What is your favorite color?") or any of a dozen other gems?

Probably the greatest single comic moment in sound films is the famous "Vessel with the pestle" sequence in Danny Kaye's *The Court Jester* (1955), certainly the best example of Agee's sequence of laughs in the era of sound. If you've seen the movie you'll know the line: "The vessel with the pestle has the pellet with the poison. The flagon with the dragon has the brew that is true." As Kaye and the knight he opposes each try to remember which cup is safe to drink out of before their duel, they learn that the vessel with the pestle has been broken and replaced with a chalice from the palace. "Just remember that," they are told. Good luck. While they struggle to remember, the shots cross-cutting from one to the other as they make their way to the jousting ground, the creators (the film was written and directed by the team of Norman Panama and Melvin Frank) add yet another complication, taking the audience farther up Agee's comic ladder. A bolt of lightning strikes Kaye's suit of armor, magnetizing it so that it keeps attracting his opponent's helmet, and then the opponent himself, till they appear as mismatched Siamese twins when they finally get to the ceremonial table where the two cups are waiting for them, each reaching for what he thinks is the unpoisoned cup.

It's an example of comic dialogue driving the scene, but with the brilliant setting — the upcoming duel — that provides the tension necessary to make it work. It is light years away from the endless succession of one-liners and quick gags that we've become accustomed to in recent years, and continues to hold up even after more than forty years.

CHAPTER 7

WHY "THE COMMITMENTS" IS THE SECOND-BEST MOVIE MUSICAL OF ALL TIME

Movie musicals are a strange construct. They're third-generation descendants of European operas, yet they never have been popular in Europe. The line of descent went from opera to operetta to Broadway musical to movie musical, and for the first ten years of their lives — the 1930s — most of them were just filmed versions of Broadway extravaganzas or popular operettas. What they offered audiences in that decade was the chance to hear glorious show tunes and — in the Fred Astaire-Ginger Rogers films — see breathtaking ballroom and tap dancing. Busby Berkeley's human-pinwheel choreography, a style that used hundreds of dancers to form changing geometric shapes, or had armies of them tapping their way up and down art-deco staircases, had a brief vogue, but survives in revivals today only as a curiosity.

But by the end of the thirties, if musicals were to survive, they had to exchange escape fantasies for emotional power. After all, no one conjures up an orchestra and bursts into song at the office, or while stopped at a traffic light. But it was a hard lesson to learn, as studios kept trying to find ways to set musical numbers in lifelike situations. The Judy Garland-Mickey Rooney films were built on school/college/summer camp platforms of the "hey, let's put on a show to raise money and save the school/college/summer camp" genre, which meant that much of the music and dance was shown as part of the supposed rehearsal and performance schedule. But it wasn't until musicals abandoned that frantic search for believability that they began to show their genius.

Let's go back a moment. The 20s and 30s were the era of great Broadway songwriters: George and Ira Gershwin, Cole Porter, Irving Berlin, Jerome Kern and Oscar Hammerstein II, Richard Rodgers and Lorenz Hart. All of them wrote musical after musical, classic song after classic song. Their shows had gorgeous melodies, witty lyrics, a lot of good jokes, and tiny, almost nonexistent plots and characters. But popular as they were on stage, when they were translated into films, audiences felt that something was missing. Broadway shows just weren't built to hold the attention of a movie audience. The spectacle was fine, but when the live theatre experience was replaced by a flat two-dimensional screen that put the audience at a remove from the action, and when it was now seen in black and white instead of the live color of Broadway (movie musicals didn't have color until 1939, with *The Wizard of Oz*), musicals disappeared from most Hollywood production schedules, with Warners and MGM left as the only studios willing to keep trying. In 1939 MGM moved its staff lyricist Arthur Freed into the role of production

Off to see the Wizard in *The Wizard of Oz.*

supervisor for musicals, and *The Wizard of Oz* was his first effort. He is credited with insisting that Judy Garland be cast as Dorothy, and he hired the team of Yip Harburg and Harold Arlen to write the songs.

And the songs! They expressed feelings, they were appropriate to the moment, they had the wit and power to go beyond the clichéd lyrics of the traditional show tune and reveal what could never be expressed in conventional dialogue. "Over the Rainbow" was the fantasy of a prepubescent girl beginning to sense the existence of a wider world, of romance, of life beyond the mundane. When, for the next thirty years, Judy Garland sang it as a nightclub showstopper she reverted to the little girl she played in the film, and got the audience response appropriate to the character they remembered from the movie. The songs defined character — "If I only had a brain..., a heart..., courage..." — and they matched the personalities who sang them. It's not too much of a stretch to say that they had a power similar to that of operatic arias in expressing their characters' emotions and conflicts. The songs of *The Wizard of Oz* are exemplars of what movie musicals can do at their best.

This was the first great musical, though I think it more rightly belongs in a category of its own — call it fantasy, or fairy tale. Its appeal is enormous, for the film is as powerful, as touching, as witty, and as important to adults as it is to children. Part of its genius is that it wastes barely a minute on setting the table. It introduces Dorothy and Toto, Uncle Henry and Aunt Em, the farmhands, Miss Gulch, and Professor Marvel, and the tornado arrives and sweeps us up into the magic. From then on, anything goes. Scarecrow, Tin Man, Cowardly Lion, Yellow Brick Road, flying monkeys, wicked witches, the Emerald City, all are as believable as though this were a documentary, because they take themselves seriously and because they have emotional power. Sixteen-year-old Judy Garland, breasts strapped tightly to her rib cage so she would appear pre-pubescent, is entirely captivating as the audience's surrogate, taking us through the amazing adventure, singing gorgeous songs in that wonderfully winsome voice, letting her emotions hang out, and triumphing by virtue of her character's farm-bred strength.

Interestingly, as the thirties ended and movie musicals faced their crisis of believability, Broadway musicals too were running out of creative energy, and it wasn't till 1943 that Broadway took a leaf from Freed's book with the Theater Guild production of *Oklahoma*. This Rodgers and Hammerstein show integrated its songs and its dances into the story, so that things didn't come

Gene Kelly, Debbie Reynolds, Donald O'Connor in *Singin' in the Rain*.

to a screeching halt when it was time for a song, but instead the show made use of the music to reveal and expand plot and character and motivation. In that sense *Oklahoma* was closer to opera than it was to previous musicals. In the forties also, a new generation of show writers came of age, particularly exemplified by the book- and lyric-writing team of Betty Comden and Adolph Green. *On the Town* was their breakthrough musical, with a story about three sailors on a weekend leave in New York. With music by Leonard Bernstein and choreography by Jerome Robbins, and a plot that integrated songs, dances, and dialogue, the show was fast, funny, and even touching in spots.

Freed recognized Comden and Green's talents too, and they did the screenplay for his MGM version of *On The Town*. They also were called in from time to time as script doctors for other writers' musicals. In all, Freed produced almost a dozen musicals between 1939 and 1952, but the one he'll always be remembered for is *Singin' in the Rain*.

The best musical

Keep in mind that a movie musical is, or should be, first a movie, and then a musical. The problem with most of them in the 1930s had been that they were musicals but not good movies. The genius of *Singin' in the Rain* is that it is first a wonderful movie, with all that that implies — script, acting, direction — and then that it has added some fine songs and brilliant dancing that are used because they enrich and illuminate both the plot and the characters. That genius begins with Comden and Green's script, full to overflowing with great gags, witty lines, and believable characters whose actions and conflicts all grow out of who they are. It continues with the direction by Gene Kelly and his partner Stanley Donen, whose task it was to shoot the film in such a way that the characters emerged as believable people from the gags, the songs, and the dances, rather than, as in so many other musicals, fighting them. And third, the casting was so right that, like the characters in *The Wizard of Oz*, it is hard to imagine anyone else playing any role in this film. The integration of all these elements invites comparison with the creation of an opera.

The plot is at once simple and sophisticated, a backstage story of the coming of sound to Hollywood. The year is 1928, and all the studios are struggling with the need to remake themselves, and their movies, to go with the new technology. Jean Hagen plays Lina Lamont, a silent-movie queen who has beauty but the most deliciously awful voice ever heard in films, and Hagen won an Academy Award for her work. Her romantic costar in the silents, Don Lockwood, played by Kelly, is smooth, handsome, sexy, and has a voice that will be just fine in the talkies. His best friend is his lifetime pal and mood music provider for his silent films, Cosmo Brown, played by Donald O'Connor. The film opens with Kelly on his way to the premiere of his and Hagen's new silent film *The Duelling Cavalier*. He meets young Debbie Reynolds, playing Kathy Selden, an aspiring actress who now works as a dancer popping out of the cake at parties, and the film is underway.

Wisely, Comden and Green involve us early with a great look back at Don and Cosmo's life as entertainers, showing us everything from the boys playing for pennies at pool halls, to their failures in vaudeville, to Don's lucky break as a stunt man in the silents. What's remarkable is that the flashback is told in song and dance, with a witty voiceover by Kelly. What's rarely mentioned in commentary about this film is just how good the flashback section is. Both the child actors who play Don and Cosmo early on, and the settings they're shown working in, are right out of a vaudeville show. Then with Kelly and O'Connor reliving their later show-business adventures, by showing us rather than just telling us, we in the audience have even grasped the essence of silent movies.

By the time we return to the present, at the premiere of *The Duelling Cavalier*, we know all we need to know about their lives and personalities and talents. We're now primed for the film's story and plot to come to us as much in song as in dialogue. No grinding halts, no lavish production numbers appearing out of nowhere. In an amazing piece of work, Comden and Green have fit their scenario and dialogue to the lyrics and moods of the songs they used in the film — songs dating from twenty and thirty years before, most of them written by Freed and his early partner Nacio Herb Brown — so that whatever the characters say, sing, or dance seems organic and proper to the film. The signature title number remains as breathtaking after dozens of viewings as it was after the first, because it is the perfect marriage of music, lyrics, choreography and dancer, and because it reflects so well the story and the character.

Throughout the film, with only one — mighty — exception, songs and dances appear at the right time, with the right motivation, to take their place along with the gags and jokes and plot twists, and deepen and enrich the film. The mighty exception, of course, is the "Broadway Rhythm" mini-film, that for reasons no one seems to recall anymore was inserted apparently to show off Kelly as having a broader range of dance talent than the film had already given us. It introduces Cyd Charisse as a young dancer's muse, dancing as Kelly's partner. Years later, he talked about it. "We had to have a number there. We never meant it to be that long [17 minutes], but since we were introducing a new character into the show, we had to keep adding to it and adding to it. It went on for hours, it seems." Today, it seems like a third foot grafted onto a dancer's leg.

Nevertheless, *Singin' in the Rain* has no peers. It is that amazing once-in-a-lifetime event every film artist wishes for, where every element works because the film has given us a half-dozen characters who are alive, believable, and are seen to act as they do out of their own personalities and conflicts. It's the funniest, wittiest (not the same thing), and most charming musical of all. Every critic has his or her favorite moments and numbers, and here is a bit of trivia for you to use on your own friends: Though Debbie Reynolds was, and is, a singer herself, she did not do her own singing in the film (she was dubbed by Betty Noyes), and the lines she supposedly dubbed for Jean Hagen's character Lina Lamont were actually dubbed by Hagen for Reynolds. Go figure.

All this praise for the integrated musical is not to demean the films of Fred Astaire and Ginger Rogers. They were brilliant dancers and good actors, whose numbers have always transported audiences with their elegance and flair, their choreography, and extraordinary talent. There never was a dancer in films to compare with Astaire, certainly not Kelly, who is clunky next to him. But Astaire's films as films never had a story or script good enough to hold our interest between the dance numbers. Plots were barely there, and there was nothing resembling characterization. The films stayed on the surface, skipping from dance cue to dance cue in a style that was almost emblematic of thirties musicals. We treasure them today for the chance to see two great artists at work, but not for the quality of their films.

The worst musical

If there's a best, there must be a worst, and not to keep you in suspense the most atrocious musical, the one that combines the greatest quantity of smarmy, infantile sentiment with the ooziest treacle of simple-minded melodies and unspeakably trite lyrics, is *The Sound of Music*. It's irrelevant that the show it's based on was the most popular musical ever produced up to that time. This is not a book about bad taste in America, but about how and why films can be seen to be good or bad.

It's easy to blame Rodgers and Hammerstein, who had written themselves out years before and were raiding the old songbook for anything they could steal and rewrite, but they wrote the songs for the Broadway show, not the movie. (The show's book was written by Howard Lindsay and Russel Crouse.) It took other hands to make the film, notably the screenwriter Ernest Lehman, who had previously taken the powerful theme and breathtaking music and lyrics of Bernstein and Sondheim's *West Side Story* and turned them into a shallow little peek at underclass life, a kind of precursor to *Welcome Back Kotter*, substituting cute jokes for valid emotion. His coworker on *The Sound of Music* was the director Robert Wise, and almost sixty years later many film people have not yet forgiven him for accepting RKO's offer to reshoot and recut parts of Orson Welles's *The Magnificent Ambersons* while Welles was on location in South America.

What did these men do? In Lehman's case not very much, because a) the show was so popular that no one in Hollywood would dare to change a thing; and b) the show's book was already in terminal paralysis from an over-load of clichés. All Lehman had to do was transpose it to film by indicating that the exteriors should be shot in Austria. For Robert Wise the verdict is more serious. Since the director has to bear the responsibility for how a film looks on screen, we can start by blaming him for the clunky opening montage of the Alps, with shaky aerial footage that alternates between shots of snowcapped peaks and low cultivated valleys, with anachronistic clearcuts visible on the hillsides, intercut with a strange shot of a broad plain, and then ending with a helicopter move across a high meadow to Julie Andrews spinning and singing and fighting to keep her balance in the wind from the rotors.

We should also blame him for all the children trying and failing to match her British accent, and ending up with lots of jaw movement and no spontaneity. If you're going to make a film with children, you have to remember that they're not simply small adults. But his inability to give us believable children is only a small part of what's wrong here. Wise was never known, in any of his films, for good visual sense, and it shows here in many ways. His scenes are always overlit. Characters supposedly shot in bright sun will generate three or four shadows on the ground around them, from the great arc lights that were the hallmark of Hollywood productions in the 50s and 60s. Wise even tries to mix and match live exteriors with studio shots against painted backdrops, and there is one ghastly moment when the camera looks past the characters on the path down to the lake, sees across the lake to the far shore, and spots three enormous geese, each the relative size of a cabin cruiser, supposedly flying along that shore but actually being pulled across the painted backdrop in some dreadfully misguided attempt at verisimilitude.

And then there is the matter of Julie Andrews. Supposedly a young novice at the abbey, she was actually 30 when the film was made and looks every day of it, particularly with a sophisticated chop to her hair and a quite inordinate amount of makeup, more than most nuns were wearing at the time. She is a good actress and a fine singer, but all the lip-syncing finally does her in, as she rarely exerts herself enough to match the energy of her voice on the sound track. Christopher Plummer does his best, keeping a stiff upper lip throughout, as befits a character written in one dimension. And there is a priceless scene in the abbey when Peggy Wood as the abbess suddenly bursts into song ("Climb Ev'ry Mountain") as a way of encouraging

Andrew Strong (age 16!) as soul singer Deco in *The Commitments*.

poor Maria to go back to Captain Von Trapp and try once more, only this time to let her feelings show. A little bonus: for those who have seen the Zucker-Abraham-Zucker film *Top Secret!* you will find out where the ballroom dance parody came from. All of which is to say that a good worst film should have something for everyone to make fun of, and *The Sound of Music* has it in spades.

A confirming note: In 1998 a group of crack-addicted monkeys in an experimental lab at the University of Minnesota were allowed to watch television. Their favorite video? *The Sound of Music.*

Meet "The Commitments"

Movie musicals traditionally have been big-budget productions, using recognized performers singing and playing well-known pieces. They are marketed strongly to the widest possible audience. In the 1990s, with Disney the only studio making them, and in animation at that, they were marketed with as many toy and fast-food tie-ins as possible to take advantage of every conceivable appeal to children. But a few times during the past twenty years an idiosyncratic British director named Alan Parker has made musicals that violated every rule of musical filmmaking. Starting out in London in the early seventies as a director of television commercials, he went to Hollywood and began making features. In 1980 he made *Fame*, about a group of students at New York's High School of Performing Arts, who sing and dance as part of their education; and *Pink Floyd: The Wall*, a strange kind of rock opera. And in 1996 he made the film of *Evita*. But Parker is not simply a director of musical films. His credits include the very bizarre *Bugsy Malone* (1976), a musical sendup of a gangster film with an all-child cast; *Midnight Express* (1978), the story of a young American imprisoned in Turkey for carrying marijuana; *Shoot the Moon* (1982), the drama of a family in the process of breaking up; and *Mississippi Burning* (1988), about the FBI investigation of a civil rights murder. Certainly he is the most versatile director working in America today, and critics are beginning to acknowledge that he may well be one of the best.

What would be a challenge for such a filmmaker? How about *The Commitments*, which he made in 1990. Here is what he did: He took a novel (and script) by the Irish writer Roddy Doyle, about a group of young Dubliners from the back streets and the projects, the underclass of the underclass, and turned it into an extraordinary movie musical. The story goes this way: A poor young Dubliner named Jimmy Rabbitte, who scratches out a living by selling bootlegged tapes and music-group T-shirts on the street, has a fixation on the great black American R&B songwriters of the 40s and 50s. He conceives the idea of starting a soul-music band to play that music, the songs of Otis Redding, Percy Sledge, Wilson Pickett, and the others. Why? Because, as he explains to the group of nondescript young singers and musicians he's put together, "The Irish are the blacks of Europe, the Dubliners are the blacks of Ireland, and the North Siders are the blacks of Dublin." He will name the band "The Commitments", because they are committed to soul music.

The film is the story of the creation, the rise, and the fall of the group — bullied, cajoled, egged on by Jimmy, the driven one, the instigator, who is not a musician himself but is their manager, their nanny, their agent, their babysitter, doing whatever it takes to give the band vitality and get some bookings. The group are all in their teens and twenties — a bus conductor, two workers in a meatpacking plant, high school and college students, one or two unemployed like Jimmy himself, one on probation for assault. And then the last addition is an older man, Joey "The Lips" Fagan, a trumpeter who says that he played in America with some of the great soul musicians years before, but has come back to Dublin to take care of his aging mother. He is both the conscience of the band and the cause of its downfall.

Does this sound like a promising concept for a movie musical? I think not. And yet Parker has found a way to show us each of the members so lovingly, and with so much wit and warmth, that we in the audience simply melt as we watch them. He's defined them well, given them distinct personalities, and made them interact on different levels so that every scene has a new insight for us to catch as we watch them. They play and sing the music themselves, so we're not distracted by post-dubbing, and they are good. Very good. The nearest thing to a name in the cast is Colm Meaney, who plays Jimmy's father, a man himself besotted with music, though for him it's the music of Elvis Presley. (There are two portraits on his living room wall. One is of Pope John Paul II, and above him is Elvis, and as far as Mr. Rabbitte is concerned that is the proper relationship of the two.)

What makes the film delicious to watch is that it is a comedy, and a very successful one. These are very witty young people, who have a thousand-year tradition of jokes, one-liners, and insults to work with as they try to learn the pieces, rehearse, and perform. They dish it out and they can take it. They are stuck with a lead singer who is one of the great slobs of motion picture history. He offends all and charms no one but himself, and yet he — young, white, fat, and obnoxious — is a great soul singer. Part of the pleasure of the film, and the tension of the plot, is watching the gap between talent and catastrophe grow narrower and narrower.

And the songs. They're an almost forgotten piece of Americana, popular only on "race" records at the time, never crossing over to the general market until white musicians began covering them in later years. They're "Mustang Sally," "Chain of Fools," "The Dark End of the Street," "Destination Anywhere," "In the Midnight Hour," and even Otis Redding's version of the treacly Bing Crosby ballad "Try a Little Tenderness," along with a dozen others. They have a beat like no other genre in popular music, and the harmonies are as gorgeous as a Mozart mass. They're erotic love songs set to the beat of a gospel choir, and they're rigid stylistically, with little variation allowed in the way they are played and sung. Just like church music, no improvising is permitted except for the lead vocalist, who is allowed to sing all around the beat. But the backup and the instruments must hit every chord and harmony as though it were church music. The songs are powerful, and they have the excitement of great gospel music — except that most of these songs are about sex.

Parker has pulled all these elements together, held them tightly as only the best directors can, enriched each scene with verbal and physical wit, and encouraged all his actors to create textured human beings who fill out their roles with unexpected depth. This is a film of a thousand pleasures, made up of the juxtaposition of believable human beings from a believable world doing something so out of character, with so much aplomb, that it all works on a level far above anything we in the audience have any right to expect. That is why it is second only to *Singin' in the Rain* as a musical.

CHAPTER 8

IS IT JUST THE LANGUAGE BARRIER, OR ARE FOREIGN FILMS REALLY BETTER?

Americans are well insulated from the terrors of having to watch foreign films. Even in World Film Central, that area in Manhattan from Houston Street to 68th & Broadway, home of more movie theatres per square block than anywhere else in the universe, most of the 'plexes show only American films. Still, if you're a New Yorker and want to see foreign films, you can find at least thirty being screened in one place or another in Manhattan on any given day. Thirty! Imagine! That's more than the *total* number of films from *anywhere at all* that are playing in any other city except Los Angeles, and there you have to drive hours and hours to get from one to another.

So it's no wonder that most of us have never so much as read a subtitle in our lives. Not only do we not speak another language, we don't even *want* to speak one. It's amazing that we're still members of the United Nations. And yet the Motion Picture Academy awards a Foreign Language Oscar every year, the newsmagazines review them, Bravo and the Independent Film Channel still run them occasionally on cable, and most cities have at least one art house that shows independent American and occasional foreign films to small audiences generally made up of local PBS and NPR station members. You could say there's an almost perfect statistical correlation between listeners to Terry Gross's NPR program *Fresh Air* and lovers of foreign films.

Nevertheless, and in spite of the common wisdom, a good number of other countries do actually make movies, some of which in fact arrive in the United States in order to be shown here. The cult of Jackie Chan's and John Woo's Hong Kong movies grew exponentially through the 90s, though their films were shot in Cantonese and Mandarin and (very badly) dubbed for the American market. *La Femme Nikita* spawned an American remake and a television series. But in general the market for foreign films seems to be made up of a) longtime film enthusiasts who remember Bergman, Fellini, and the New Wave; and b) recent college graduates who took a film appreciation course that treated both foreign and American films equally. Type a) is best defined by the famous scene in *Annie Hall* where Woody Allen and Diane Keaton arrive two minutes late at the theatre showing Marcel Ophuls's four-and-a-half-hour documentary *The Sorrow and the Pity*, about French collaboration with the Nazis in World War II, and Allen refuses to go in because the film has already started. Keaton doesn't get it, since this is not the first time they've seen the movie, but for the true film buff, coming in late is the unforgivable sin. Type b), the college student, takes the course from a faculty member who is type a), naturally, so the evolutionary line is perpetuated.

One other point. Foreign films are not quite the same as foreign *language* films. America currently welcomes many films from Australia, New Zealand, Great Britain, and (English) Canada, but as ethnocentric viewers we find an interesting fact about them, namely that even though we have a more-or-less common language, we have quite different sensibilities and even mores. No one in the United States has yet made a film about urban Indians that has the power and frankness of the New Zealand film *Once Were Warriors*, which is about a contemporary Maori family living in an urban white world. Nor have we made our *Trainspotting*, or even *The Commitments*. All made in English, easily understood, but none have entered the mainstream of film distribution.

What's true for English-language foreign films is even more true for foreign language films. They *never* get mass distribution. Is that strange? Yes, because in almost every other country in the world, films in languages other than one's own are quickly subtitled or dubbed and distributed identically to those made in the host country. Certainly it's true that American films have the largest worldwide market, but any city in France, Italy, Spain, Germany, or the Scandinavian countries will have a cosmopolitan smorgasbord of films to offer on any given day. And it's not as though the United States won't allow foreign films in. The 2000 Seattle International Film Festival presented more than 170 foreign language films, along with a hundred English-language films, during its 24-day run. But Seattle, like New York, is an aberration in America. It is a city that adores film, in fact spends more per capita on film admissions than any other community in the country, including New York. For many Seattleites, life and work are put on hold during the festival's run, which is all well and good, but you could not duplicate it in Cleveland, say, a city the same size as Seattle, or even San Francisco, which hosts the oldest film festival in the country.

Be all that as it may, the fact is that foreign films do get shown here, they do have an audience of people who care about movies as an art form, and the question is — and has been since the 1950s — what makes foreign films so good? There are three answers.

Answer No. 1: The (lack of) Money

The American film business has one bottom line: make money or die. It has been willing to throw uncounted millions (up to $200 million per film by 2000) at supposed blockbuster films, betting ever-increasing amounts in the hope that bigger would be more profitable. Other countries haven't been blessed (or cursed) with so much capital. Until recently two million dollars was a large production budget, ten million a bonanza. So filmmakers couldn't rely on special effects, on computerized morphing or animatronic characters, or anything else so exotic. It's as though novelists found their writing paper rationed, so every word had to be well thought out beforehand; or composers could write only for chamber ensembles; or painters couldn't do wall-size installations because paint cost too much. When artists — in any country, in any art form — are confronted with issues like these, issues that affect the mechanics of their work but not directly their artistic vision, they find ways to make their statements using whatever resources they have at hand. Here's an example: In the year 1963, Ingmar Bergman made two of his most powerful films (*Winter Light* and *The Silence*), Federico Fellini made his signature film *8-½*, Kurosawa made two films, Godard made three films, and the rest of the industrious members of the French New Wave made another 14 films, all for a total cost of far less than one American studio spent that year to make one film — *Cleopatra* — which cost a then-unheard-of $44 million. And unlike *Cleopatra*, at least a few of those films have stayed in the repertory as classics.

Another part of this answer is that the studios in most other countries are structured differently from those in the United States. Actors, writers and directors are rarely put under contract for more than one film at a time; they come to studios and investment partnerships for production money, and the deals are made on a picture-by-picture basis. In some countries the government will have a revolving investment fund that can be used to help meet any shortfall in private money, or even as seed money to help attract private investors.

Why would the government do this? Films that succeed around the world bring cash back in. Industries like film have a heavy capital investment in equipment, studio space, and laboratory facilities, and having them stand idle is not an option. Government participation or subsidization helps level the playing field when a country's films are distributed in competition with those of the United States. Where American distributors charge theatre owners up to 95% of the gross of a film as the price for showing it (the theatres make their money on concession sales), import distributors rarely charge more than 60%, and more commonly 35%.

And then there is the question of salaries. While American stars now get up to $20 million per picture just for showing up, or alternatively may get a percentage of the worldwide gross, actors in other countries cannot command those salaries. The out-of-pocket costs to make a film in, say, Brazil are negligible compared with even the smallest U.S. studio production. On the other hand, the American studios are not completely stupid about this. They have formed or bought subsidiaries and subsidiaries of subsidiaries whose sole function is to bankroll American independent films in exchange for worldwide distribution rights. They feel, rightly, that if they hit on only one out of five films they underwrite, they will make a profit. To date, interestingly, few of these ventures have made money for the studios, mainly because they've backed a lot of losers. Why? Probably because they search for the new rather than the good.

Answer No. 2: The Art Form

Most feature films in the United States are made the way they are because most films that were made before them were made the same way. Conventions of style, look, and structure become guidelines to be followed by successive filmmakers, sometimes morphing into rules, and then into absolute mandates. Historically, this came about because most American films were made in the studios or with studio backing, and studio money people feel uncomfortable when rules are broken. So, they would say, if you want the dough for your film, here's the way you have to make it. Even today, the producer, not the director, has the final say in Hollywood. The directors who get carte blanche from their studios or backers can be listed on the fingers of your hands: Lucas, Spielberg, Tarantino, James Cameron, and the Coen brothers come to mind. And none of them is noted for cerebral, intellectual work. The nearest any of them have come to a thoughtful, issue-based film, Spielberg's *Schindler's List*, was, first, adapted from Thomas Keneally's well-known novel, and second, tied in with the deal he made to direct the *Jurassic Park* films for the studio. Cameron's *Titanic*, the adventure romance to end all adventure romances, was in 1997 the most expensive film ever made, at more than $200 million. It's already paid its nervous studio backers a fortune in profits, but it caused much heart failure before it was finished. It's the quintessential Hollywood film, the one that actually got to where everyone else only hoped to go by throwing money at a script, and to judge by past performance it will just open the gates to more studio films like it.

But most other countries, with the exception of India, Hong Kong, and for a while Japan, have not had such a controlling studio structure. They don't turn out hundreds of films each year, they don't have exclusive contracts for their creative people, and they serve mostly as suppliers of money, production facilities, and distribution contacts for films as they are made, one by one, by independent filmmakers. Over the years this has given the filmmakers a great deal of control over their own work — far more than most American filmmakers get. And while the ratio of good artists to mediocre is surely no greater in other countries than it is in the United States, the best artists make only what they want to make, the way they want to make it, without studio interference.

They can do this because the timeline for recouping production costs is much longer in other countries than it is in the United States. Production investors, whether studios or government funds, are accustomed to waiting a while for their returns. Selection for screening at film festivals, and getting awards and honors, are much more important because they translate directly into grosses, while no festival or award would have any effect on, say, the grosses of Spielberg's *The Lost World*. The same is true for favorable critical notice. Countries that can boast of major filmmakers, whose work is studied and screened by thoughtful intellectuals and academics, and written about in film journals, will reap the reward of long-term box-office success for those artists' films. And because the financial nut is so small, even one favorable review, by one critic in one newspaper or magazine in just one country, can have an impact on the worldwide gross of a film. In America, the first weekend's grosses determine whether a film lives or dies.

All that having been said, however, there is one overriding reason why foreign films are at least different from American ones, and often enormously better, and that is that in other countries of the world film is taken seriously as an art form. Filmmakers are treated in much the same way as novelists or composers or sculptors. Their work is discussed, thought about, studied, analyzed, and set in context. Filmmakers are expected to take their own work seriously too, and not treat it simply as "product." They are trusted as a novelist is trusted, to create characters, relationships, motivations, and conflicts built on an artist's understanding of real and believable personalities. To the extent that they succeed, their films will be better than ours. Where the creation of an American film like *The Godfather* is seen as an exception, almost an aberration, in the studio system, it is rather the rule in other countries. Our films are seen by those who pay for them as entertainments rather than art. But when Ingmar Bergman and Akira Kurosawa, Federico Fellini and François Truffaut were making films, no one would have dared to change their scripts, specify their casts, or tell them how to shoot. And as filmmakers in dozens of countries in Africa, Asia, and Latin America begin to draw worldwide attention, their backers are unlikely to be any more demanding.

This is not to say that politics and governmental policies don't play a role in, or even control, the films of certain countries. China is notorious for denying funding and distribution to filmmakers it finds have made offensive films, and it is by no means alone. All dictatorships and most authoritarian governments practice censorship of one form or another, and it is most visible in a medium like film. This is not new, of course. Filmmakers have been exiled and worse for a hundred years, and we can only imagine the worth of films not made and careers cut short or abandoned.

Nevertheless, films get made and filmmakers make them. And as with any art form there are certain elements that give a film some lasting value, some resonances that tell of an artist's conjunction with important questions, whether personal or philosophical. They're the elements that help give the work its chance at greatness. The Metropolitan Museum's famous self-portrait by Rembrandt as an aging, homely man is so riveting, so filled with information about himself and us, about his mind and our minds, about his humanity and ours, that we can come back to it for a lifetime and never exhaust it. Has there been an American painting anywhere near so powerful? Not yet. How come? Well, certain forms of death are closer to those who grow up in other countries than they are to those who grow up here. It's as though the Rembrandt in the painting has seen more of life and death than those of us who come to it in the museum. Unlike most of the rest of the world, the United States hasn't been physically touched by war in almost a hundred fifty years, and lucky as we are, we pay the price in an innocence of artworks and a huge market for fantasy. It would be very difficult for a Guatemalan filmmaker, or a Rwandan or a Russian, for example, to make a cops-and-robbers, spies-and-counterspies, fantasy musical or shoot-em-up, even if they had the money and facilities. It's not in their vocabulary. What is in their vocabulary is war, dislocation, fragmented lives and relationships, and perhaps a greater experience of trauma than an American has had. Truffaut's film *Jules and Jim* is a great romance, a witty and beautiful triangle of two men and a woman. But what underlies the romance is war and death; the film's great dislocation is World War I, with two protagonists on one side and one on the other. And the film finds its ending at the time of the Nazis' book burning. It is not a film that an American could have made.

For Ingmar Bergman, war and its consequences, intended and unintended, direct and indirect, have been important in many of his films. *The Seventh Seal* is about a knight in the twelfth century who comes home, exhausted, from another failed crusade. But the movie is not about the crusades, nor the clash of religions and cultures, nor even war at all. As the knight rests on the beach of his homeland, the figure of death comes to claim him. But the knight, who has never run from death on the battlefield, says to this figure, this inexorable gatherer of souls, that before he dies he must find out for himself whether there is any hope for mankind, any innocence, any life force left in the world, ultimately whether his own life had any meaning. So to buy time he challenges death to a game of chess. They agree that as long as the game goes on, the knight survives to pursue his quest. The rest of the film shows us what he finds in his search.

Answer No. 3: The Problem of Translation

Could *The Seventh Seal* have been made by an American? The crusades are not even in our vocabulary. What is in our vocabulary is the Civil War, but even there the definitive film has yet to be made. An interesting American phenomenon is the art that came out of the Depression. In films it was fantasy, not realism. Neither filmmakers nor audiences were interested in portraits of life at the time. Few films were made of the Hoovervilles, the urban dislocations, the long lines of unemployed, the stunted children. The closest was Steinbeck's *The Grapes of Wrath*, both novel and film, and without demeaning the power of the story we have to say that it lacks the resonance of great art.

By contrast, during the years from 1945 to 1950, Italian filmmakers turned out more than a dozen remarkable studies of their own country as it emerged from fascism to face a new postwar world. These were not socialist-realist films in the exhortative, Stalinist style. The filmmakers were called neo-realists, and their films dealt with individuals and families confronting dislocations and hardships beyond anything they had previously dreamed of. Since that time, all filmmakers dealing with transcendent issues like war and its aftermath have lived with being compared to the neo-realists and their work.

Which is not to say that there is an absence of wit or humor or sophisticated treatment of life, at any level, in films from other countries. We don't see as much of it here because a lot of comedy doesn't translate as well as drama does, and distributors tend to bring "statement" films, or those with an "adult" theme, into this country before they bring in comedies. Juzo Itami's *Tampopo* is an example of a comedy that made a great success here (by foreign-film standards); Buñuel's *The Discreet Charm of the Bourgeoisie* is another. Obviously, comedies are popular around the world, but only certain types can cross international borders. The thrust and parry of sophisticated conversation, the essence of a film like the American classic *All About Eve*, for example, is going to have a hard time at the box office in, say, Japan.

The reverse is also true. For other than special audiences, literate in the language and culture of the filmmaker, eyes that dart incessantly from action to subtitle for two hours at a time are more than most Americans expect to provide a foreign filmmaker with. But it's the reason we dismiss foreign films out of hand and thereby deny ourselves the chance to meet some great art. We seem to be insular jingoists at heart, and we don't show much inclination to change.

CHAPTER 9

WHAT ALL THE OTHER OSCARS ARE ABOUT

Here are the things we pay attention to when we go to the movies: The actors, the dialogue, the action, the plot. Here are the things we don't pay attention to: The cinematography, the editing, the music, the casting, the set design and art direction, and the special effects. Well, maybe we pay attention to the special effects, particularly if that's why we went to see the film, but a lot of movies that were built around special effects, like 1998's big bombs *Armageddon*, *Godzilla*, and *Deep Impact*, were films that you couldn't pay people to see. Nevertheless, the caliber and imagination of all these arts and crafts are important, sometimes crucial, to the quality and resonance of their films. Here's an overview.

Cinematography
The one person on the set or location of any film who knows more about everything than anyone else is the cinematographer, also known as the director of photography, or D.P. for short. He or she knows the following: the mechanics of how a camera works; the physics of light that passes through the lens and shutter and is focused so as to make an image on the film; the ways in which different lenses lengthen or foreshorten or distort those images; the chemistry of film emulsions that record the image for later development at the lab; the best choice and positioning and intensity and focus of lights, reflectors, scrims, and cutters (devices that block light, soften it, or cast shadows across something in the shot) so as to achieve the effect desired by the director; the right type of camera mount or crane or dolly or helicopter to use in order to make the shot work the way the director wants;

and about a thousand other pieces of useful information that will help the movie look better, or more interesting, or more exciting. The cinematographer knows who looks best in what colors, styles, or makeup, and often can be better than the director at composing shots so that they communicate the right mood or feeling of a scene to the audience. In addition, the D.P. hires the key crew members; they and their assistants work for the D.P., not the director or producer, though the production pays their salaries.

There's a long route to becoming a cinematographer, particularly if you're in the union. You'll start by spending time as a loader — loading and unloading film magazines that will be run through the camera. You'll do it in a darkroom in the studio sound stage, or in a special lightproof bag on location, working by feel alone because any light — even the tiniest bit — can ruin the film. Step two is to become a focus puller. You'll sit or stand or run next to the camera as it moves close to or farther away from the actors, changing the focal point of the lens so as to keep them in focus. You'll also keep the lenses and the camera movement clean and free from schmutz, grease, fingerprints, or bits of film emulsion. Step three is to become the camera operator, the one who turns the camera on and off and actually looks through the eyepiece and turns, pans, or tilts the camera during the shot. He or she must then tell the cinematographer and director whether there were any glitches, any bumps, any jarring, or any moments in which the camera was not positioned exactly where it was wanted. The operator also must notice whether a microphone or boom appears in the shot, or whether some extra far away in the background wasn't where he or she was supposed to be. These days most features use a video camera coupled to the film camera's lens, so the director and the D.P. can check each take before approving it. Still, it's up to the operator to spot any possible trouble.

At this point in one's career it's a good idea to spend a lot of time hanging around the lighting people and learning all about what lights go where and why, because the real job of the cinematographer is not to shoot the film but to light it, and to light it creatively and appropriately. When the director says, "I want this scene to look mysterious," it's expected that a) the cinematographer will know just what kind of "mysterious" the director means, i.e., mysterious scary, mysterious puzzling, mysterious cosmic, or mysterious other; and b) the cinematographer will know exactly how to light it for that effect. When the film is a nineteenth-century costume drama, it's expected that the cinematographer will know how to light the sets so they appear to be lit with gas lamps. For the eighteenth century it's candles. For the twenty-fifth it's — who knows? And so on.

Where do camera operators go from here? If they're lucky and good, they may get hired to be the director of photography on the second or third unit of a feature film, shooting locations or inserts or other footage that doesn't require the presence of the stars or director or cinematographer. Their eye and lighting and shot composition will be carefully scrutinized by producers, directors, and cinematographers for signs of talent or even genius. On the other hand, what they're given to shoot is usually storyboarded and tightly controlled, so there isn't much room for imagination. It's a conundrum, but at some point, with enough talent and luck, there can be a breakthrough.

The breakthrough comes with being chosen to shoot a feature as cinematographer. It's usually low budget and low pay, because otherwise a well-known D.P. would have been hired. And because cinematographers rarely can or want to pick and choose, working only on films of one particular type, they had better be good — they had better be great — at everything. When they are, or when they show promise of becoming great, then they'll enter the select group that shoots most of the big studio films. A little exercise for you, as you watch a movie, is to try and place yourself in the position of the camera, and see the film as the director and D.P. do. Notice the lighting, the camera moves, the choice of focus and concentration on one or another actor or object, and see whether you think they might have done better. You should do this because it will help you understand that that's what they get paid for, and that's what separates the ordinary from the great or even good. Ask yourself if you would have shot the scene as they did; think about alternate camera positions, or different moves, or different lighting. After all, they do that, for every shot in the film.

In recent years a number of well-known D.P.s have gone on to direct their own films. Sometimes it works, sometimes it doesn't. There isn't always a correlation between what the shot looks like and what the film is about, and not all cinematographers understand that. People who have spent twenty years lighting and shooting scenes don't always have the skills to edit scripts, cast actors, and direct performances.

Editing

Editing was the first film craft to allow, even honor and encourage, women, who have now been at the top of the editing world, equal to men, since the days of silent films. Ann V. Coates edited a number of David Lean's films, including *Lawrence of Arabia*. Thelma Schoonmaker has been Martin Scorsese's editor for many years. Dede Allen edited *Bonnie and Clyde*. Other examples abound, and the reason is that editors, by the nature of the job, worked far from the macho shenanigans of crews on traditional film sets and locations, and so they were spared the putdowns and humiliations that women on the set were subject to. Editors were and are valued for their work, not their gender.

So how does an editor work? Simply put, the editor begins by taking the footage that's been shot and printed at the lab each day, and assembles selected shots and takes into a rough version of what each scene should look like, adding more and more scenes as the film is shot, then putting them into the proper sequence (the death before the funeral, the wedding before the divorce), until he or she ends up with a rough cut of the final complete movie. In a sense that's true, but the reality is much more complex, and more interesting.

The editor's job is basically to work with the director and turn the footage that's been shot into a movie, a movie that has value and impact, that takes its characters from one place to another, with growth or change or development along the way, that has a plot, that holds together, that's worth watching. All this means constantly making choices. In any worthwhile film it will be necessary to make thousands of choices, beginning with the choice of which take to use out of the, say, three or five or ten or more that were printed of each shot during yesterday's shoot. Here's an example. There are four people in an office, discussing a plan that one of them has proposed. Each of them has something to say, starting with the proposer. Then each of them has a reaction to the plan. Then there's an argument between two of them about the plan, and each of the other two has a reaction to the argument. Maybe one of them leaves, in anger, and the others react to that. How would you edit that scene?

Let's go back to the shoot. The director may want to begin by establishing the location and the people. He or she can do this with, say, a wide-angle shot that includes all four characters. A more interesting way might be to begin with a shot of the person whose office it is, then have us hear a door open, move the camera to show the others entering, then watch them choose places to sit or stand. All this time there's dialogue as well. Then — do we want to focus on the person offering the plan? Do we want to see the reactions of the others as they hear it? Do we want to foreshadow the coming argument? Are the actors good enough to let the audience understand their emotions even when they're not talking? If so, do we want to show them? Or should the reaction be a surprise to the audience? Should we gradually speed up the intercutting from one to the other so as to build tension? Would that be too trite?

Enough, already. Most directors these days shoot in what you might call the American studio style. Each scene will have a master shot, of most or all of the participants, in which all moves and dialogue from beginning to end will be seen and recorded. Then each actor will have the whole scene — or their part in it — reshot as a closeup, where they will match their moves and reactions and dialogue to the master shot. Four actors, four closeups. Then the director may want to intercut "two-shots", or "three-shots", that is, shots that include only two or three of the four actors, again matching moves and dialogue. Then, let's say, one of the actors may pick up and play with a desktop object during the scene. The director may want a closeup, or insert, of that as well. The director may make as many as fifteen or twenty takes of each shot, and select any number of them to be printed at the lab and sent to the editor. How many will be printed? Usually any number from two to five, though some idiosyncratic directors will print a dozen.

All of these shots are given to the editor, along with the separately recorded sound track. Actually, for most, though not all, films these days, all the selected takes, after they're developed at the lab and coded with identifying numbers and matched with the sound takes, are recorded onto computer disks, along with the sound track for each, so as to make editing easier on special editing machines that can call up any shot from anyplace in the film, and have it appear instantly on the editing screen. It's called "offline editing." One notable exception is the work of Michael Kahn, who edits Steven Spielberg's films. Kahn and Spielberg edit on a Moviola, a wonderful old staple of the film business that's been around since the 1920s, on which you can look at the actual footage frame by frame as it moves past the viewer from reel to reel. You cut the film by actually marking the print, then taping the end of one shot to the beginning of the next, then looking at how the two cut together. The new computer-based editing machines do the same thing and do it faster, but there the editor works with a computer-generated image of the shot rather than the actual shot itself. For some editors, and most films, there's no discernible difference in the outcome, but in a 1998 interview with *The New York Times*, Kahn said, "Steven likes the smell of film. He likes to feel it, hold it. He doesn't want to look at a monitor. He also likes the idea of the Moviola [because] this is how so many great movies were made." He added that the images on the Moviola, in contrast to computers, "are better, sharper, more focused."

Regardless of the technology used — and remember that some takes that work visually may have sloppy line readings, or vice versa — the editor picks and chooses his or her way among the takes until the scene has coherence, a beginning, middle, and end that will in turn lead on to the next scene in the film. Some directors want to be intimately involved in the editing, some do not. The Directors Guild of America gives all its directors the right of what's called the first cut — the finished film as the director wants it to look. A few directors have the right of final cut, where the studio cannot touch a frame of it, or even suggest a change, without the consent of the director. Most do not, though, and many films are recut, even reshot — sometimes with a different director — after preview screenings that point to problems.

Most features also have sound editors, whose job it is to make sure that not only the dialogue but all other sounds — explosions, cars, planes, footsteps, and music come to mind — are appropriately a part of the finished film. Both the sound editor and the film's editor will work with a whole host of technicians, each of whom specializes in just one or two areas of sound creation, recording, and mixing. Sometimes if a take looks good but sounds bad, or muffled, or there was an extraneous noise that can't be removed, the actor will be called back to overdub or loop that piece of dialogue again, lip-syncing it to the footage already shot.

Music

Spike Lee's 1998 film *He Got Game* is about a black high school basketball star from the Brooklyn ghetto, and his father, who's in jail for murder. For the music in it, Lee used pieces composed many years ago by Aaron Copland, the contemporary classical composer who wrote "Appalachian

Spring," "Fanfare for the Common Man," "El Salon Mexico," and many other works that had no relation to anything or anyone in the movie. Yet the music was an inspired choice by Lee, for it has an agony and a beauty and an exaltation that give great weight to the events of the film, and add enormously to its power.

Power and emotion are what music gives to the movies, and has almost since their inception. In 1908 Camille Saint-Saëns wrote the background music for a film called *The Assassination of the Duc de Guise*. It was played, of course, by live musicians sitting in front of the screen, as was all movie music until the coming of sound with its synchronous sound track that was matched to the picture. In the silent era music filled the void left when the loudest sounds in the theatre otherwise would have been the projector motor and the comments of the audience. The big movie theatres had full orchestras and conductors, and even small towns had a pianist who played a marked score, matching each scene, that underlined or enhanced the mood of the film as it was projected. The music was a pastiche of original themes and classic or near-classic pieces, held together by various riffs or vamps that bridged the big moments. If you've seen *Singin' in the Rain* you know that the studios even had musicians, sometimes whole bands, that played mood music for the actors while the films were being shot.

And then sound came in. Interestingly, for other than musicals, the earliest talkies didn't use much music; film studios were feeling their way and concentrated on dialogue and sound effects. But by 1932 Max Steiner was composing the music for the John Barrymore-Katharine Hepburn drama *A Bill of Divorcement*, and from then on no film left its studio without music. Composers ran their own music departments, with house musicians who made their careers just playing in the studio orchestra. If MGM was not recording that day, the musicians would be over at Warner's or Columbia. For the composers and orchestrators there was little lead time; they had to get the themes down, orchestrate them — sometimes an hour's worth of original music — time them to the second, so as not to miss any cues, and then record them with the orchestra to match the scenes as they were played back on a screen. In his career Steiner composed and conducted the scores for more than 200 films, the most famous being *Gone With The Wind*, with its famous "Tara" theme.[2]

[2] Oddly enough, the theme is hardly heard at all during the movie itself; it plays under the opening and closing credits at full strength, was instantly a hit, and came to define the movie.

The current composing star is John Williams, who by 1998 had won Academy Awards for *Jaws*, *Star Wars*, *E.T.*, and *Schindler's List*, and been nominated for twenty-five more. He has the ability to create memorable themes and motifs, without overpowering the films themselves, and his orchestrations — knowing when to let the brass lead, where to keep the strings muted, how best to use the woodwinds — are a valuable, if underappreciated, part of his work.

Today it's a rare film that doesn't use music in one way or another, whether composed or simply licensed — called source music — from other composers and performers. Characters listen, sing along with, dance to, have sex, or even kill, while appropriate songs are heard on the sound track. Those songs and performances often are used to set the date of the film's story, or the location in which they're heard, or the personalities and musical tastes of the characters listening to them. Mainly, though, source music creates a mood of authenticity — this is a documentary, the music seems to say. When Orson Welles's 1958 film *Touch of Evil* was restored in 1998 by the editor Walter Murch, working from a long-lost memo that Welles had written after the studio recut his film, one major change was made in the famous opening tracking shot: the film now runs without the titles added by RKO, and without the Henry Mancini music theme; his music has been replaced by what Welles originally specified: music heard on the car radio, plus music coming from the cantinas and shops along the street. We don't need the titles, nor Mancini's music either. Welles's shot had deliberately included numbers of tinny loudspeakers outside the shops, as the sources for the music. Replacing it with a composed theme on the sound track only weakened the power of the shot.

Today, many film producers commission songs to be written and performed on the film's sound track, usually under the credits, to represent the film to a wider audience. The song itself is marketed to coincide with the film's release, in the hope that it will a) make some extra money for the studio; and b) generate more film admissions than the movie might otherwise get. Occasionally it works, though mostly the song is irrelevant to the film's success or failure. However, the performances of Oscar-nominated songs do constitute a major time-filler at the Academy Awards, allowing the show to run more than three hours and generating more sponsor advertising revenue for the network and the Academy.

Recent technical advances have allowed movie music to be composed and performed, even orchestrated, on a computer. In that case only one live person is needed to do it all, but the theory and the function of the music remain the same: to add to the emotional impact of the film.

Production Design and Art Direction

From trailer trash to Trump Tower, people live and work and play in a lot of different places, and if you're going to make a movie about them you'd better design your sets to match the characters. If the movie is contemporary, you probably have lots of real-life models to borrow from. But what about the past? How did a Cincinnati retail store look in 1850? A West African village in 1400? A men's club in Edwardian London? And then there's the future, incorporating both earth and other planets, to say nothing of other galaxies. Some filmmakers and designers go retro into that good night; *Dune* comes to mind. Some go techno; space ships require it. Some try to have it both ways; *Brazil* was an example.

When a film has been cleared by the studio, the production designer will sit down with the director, the script, and the budget, and discuss the look of the film. Is it contemporary? A comedy? Sophisticated? Casual? Are the sets and locations important, or are they simply places where events happen? Does it matter whether the bedspreads are modern or traditional? What kind of furniture should the apartment have? Do they eat at Spago or at Denny's? Are the characters going to wear clothing that will snag on sharp corners? Will the chase be shot in alleys and back yards or up and down the tenement stairwells? Do they live in a Tudor mansion or a postmodern beach house?

The production designer will make notes on these and about a thousand other questions, and then start putting together his or her ideas for sets and location exteriors. Usually these ideas will be sketched out and gone over with the director and producer. They'll all meet with the location scouts to look at slides or video footage of potential locations, and visit the most likely ones. If a house or other building needs to be rented for the shoot, as opposed to building it on the stage or back lot, this is the time to make that decision. Is this a science-fiction film? If so, what should people and places look like? What will the actors have to do in and around the sets? Can an existing building serve for a film set in the future? The 1997 film *Gattaca* used the Marin County Civic Center as the headquarters for a futuristic intergalactic corporation. It saved a bundle in set construction costs.

When construction starts on sets and props, the production designer works with the art director on the look and decor of all of them. What kinds of paintings should be on the wall? Sconces or floor lamps for light? Wallpaper or paint? What style furniture? Maybe there's a schoolroom set. Old or new? Dirty or clean? Blackboard or whiteboard? Is there a barn? For horses or for cows? Painted? Unpainted? Hayloft? You get the idea. You might say that the art director is responsible for everything that isn't nailed down, from furniture to props. He or she will shop for tchotchkes, fabrics, items of all kinds and sizes, then try them out for the director and production designer. When everything is approved, the sets are built, finished, painted, and decorated, and will be ready when the crew comes to shoot. Naturally no one works alone; there are carpenters, electricians, and prop people who do the construction and assembly; they're usually career people, very skilled and experienced at what they do.

Casting

Though there are no Oscars as yet for casting directors, they now have their own professional guild, and rightly so. Hounded by agents and producers to select certain favorites and/or needy actors for every film, they can often make the difference between a movie with texture and impact and one that falls flat. Casting directors work with the director and producer to choose everyone in the film with a speaking role except the stars, who usually come to the producing studio with the package of script, producer, and director. They can audition hundreds of actors for certain parts, look at thousands of head shots or video footage for others. They work with budgets, and usually have to negotiate with agents for fees and compensation rates. The ideal casting director is someone who appreciates actors, has the intuition to choose the right one for the right part, has the balls to say no while under extreme pressure to say yes, can read a script and visualize the film and each role in it, both as the director will see it and as the audience will see it, and then can deliver the entire cast on or under budget. They'll spend days, sometimes weeks, with the director, auditioning actors or looking at video footage of them.

Good casting directors get to know and like the directors they work with, and directors are well advised to listen to their suggestions, because they have at their fingertips great numbers of actors who would shine in the right part if given the chance. They also know who's reliable and who's not, who's available and who's not, and just what the bottom dollar line is for everybody. They make friends with directors even when they're not working with them by suggesting actors for consideration. Then if the actor is a success in the role the casting director will have scored some important points. Conversely, if an actor is causing trouble on the set, the casting director may have to be called in to deal with it.

Special Effects

Certainly scores, probably hundreds, of books have been written about the how and how-to of special effects, and this is not one of them. People forget that special effects are as old as the art form; the very first movies made in the 1890s had dissolves and superimpositions and double exposures in them. From early on, filmmakers could make characters and objects appear out of nowhere and disappear from the middle of the frame. They could run film through the camera backward as well as forward, slower than normal, faster than normal, or one frame at a time, all of which produced different effects. They could put one person's head on another person's body, or even on a sheep or cow. In 1902 Georges Méliès flew people to the moon on a rocket ship. What we see today at the movies is either a) a variation and technological improvement on the optical film devices of the early years; or b) a computer-generated effect such as morphing.

The first thing to be said about a), film effects, is that they are not very expensive to do in the context of a feature film's budget. The first thing to be said about b), computer generated effects, is that they are very expensive in the context of a feature film's budget or even a country's gross national product, though the costs are coming down as fast as new software with better algorithms comes on the market, to create the effects more quickly and with less required computer power.

There's actually a third kind of special effect, and has been since the invention of films, and that is models. The original *King Kong* used models of the Empire State Building, and flew miniature airplanes around it. Today models can move, hop, run, and crush things, usually people or buildings, and are controlled by radio or computer in very complex motions. They're called "animatronic models." Often they're combined with computer-generated images to enhance the effect. Lots of technique, lots of time to create them, and lots of money. But let's remember that some of the *Star Wars* fighters were models flown along a string and filmed against a blue screen that was later replaced optically with a painted background image and actual film footage.

Probably the best use of a computer-generated shot in recent live-action filmmaking is the aerial tracking shot that James Cameron used early in the film *Titanic*, which begins with a closeup of Leonardo DiCaprio standing at the prow of the ship as it heads west into the Atlantic. The camera pulls back away from him, as though mounted on a helicopter, to see more of the ship, then it tracks in the air the length of the whole ship — that is, the ship sails past by this magic helicopter — until we watch from somewhere high in the air as the stern moves on past us, on its voyage into the setting sun, toward America. It's a shot that could never have been done before computer-generated imaging reached maturity and opened the door to entirely new ways of using film. The 1996 *Toy Story* was the first completely computer-generated movie, a kind of "virtual-reality" film where everything from its three-dimensional characters to backgrounds to action of all kinds was produced in the computer. Until those images were transferred frame by frame to optical film, they existed only on the monitors of the production company's computers.

Animated films, of course, form their own genre and have a long and honorable tradition of their own. In the 1990s, though, animators who used to work methodically, frame by frame, on acetate cells, began to take advantage of computer-assisted design programs that now give them a greater freedom to move their drawn and painted figures through scenes and actions that would have been excruciatingly difficult to animate before. Computers also let animators create backgrounds for action more quickly, and try out a variety of moves and looks before committing them to film.

CHAPTER 10

ALL YOU'LL EVER NEED TO KNOW ABOUT CREDITS

You've stayed through the end credits and now maybe you're a little curious about what the gaffer, the best boy, and the grip all did on the movie, or whether they're just involved in some sadomasochistic cult that's headquartered at the studio. In a minute. We'll get to them, along with Foley artists, wranglers, and second second assistant assistants, but first let's talk about ego. Movies are a gamble. In the movie business success has many fathers and mothers, and so does failure. Since nobody knows (well, they may *think* they know) how the film will do, everybody wants to receive their just desserts. Credits aren't really there for the audience. They're there so the industry will know who did what on the film. It will help with future jobs, with better contracts, with more deals, and obviously with getting more money next time. Credits are where the agent earns his or her money, because it's the agent who negotiates the credits.

Here's where the credit business starts: Draw a horizontal line. That line is an accountant's way of describing the costs of making a movie. Above the line go all the names of the creative people involved, along with the pay or compensation they're going to get. Who are the creative people? They're the ones with agents. They are the director, the producers, the writers, the stars and featured actors, and (these days) the production designers, composers, casting directors, and cinematographers. Below the line go all the production people — the crew members — and the out-of-pocket costs of making the movie, like allocations for location rentals, building sets, purchasing or renting equipment, getting props, recording and editing the sound track, buying film stock and processing it in the laboratory, generating the optical and special effects (now often up to half the total production cost) and the like. The line is not a figure of speech. Every production is described as consisting of above-the-line and below-the-line costs.

Now the fun begins. Who should be listed first and who shouldn't? Not to worry. Everything has already been worked out for you. With a few exceptions, here's the order. The very first credit you see on the screen, just after the lights go down and the theatre informs you that this is the feature presentation and you are fortunate enough to hear it in one or another version of Dolby sound, is the name of the studio (Buena Vista, Columbia, Universal), followed by the name of the production company that actually made the film (Amblin), followed by the name of the investment group that hopes to make a fortune by backing the film, for example a group of dentists in Minneapolis (Whitecaps IV), usually credited as "in association with." Then the director's first credit, usually "a film by (your name here)", or "a (your name) film." Then come the stars, and then comes the film's title. Sometimes the stars' and director's credits will be reversed, depending on the star's deal with the studio. Then (often) the featured actors, followed by the key production people — the casting director, composer of music, production designer, editor, director of photography, and then. . .

And then it gets sticky. We come to the writers and producers (the director will always get the final credit). The film *Quiz Show* listed eleven producers in the opening credits, although in fact there were fourteen, but three had asked to have their names removed. *Variety*'s story reported that "it required several weeks to work out a viable device for listing all the credits — which would be co-producers, executive producers, 'also produced by' producers and so forth. When one refused to go along with the settlement, the entire 'grid' had to be painstakingly reconstructed." Since no film requires eleven producers, much less fourteen, we can be pretty sure that we're seeing ego at work. Who are they all? Often they're friends, relatives, personal trainers, or other hangers-on of the star, whose names are added on as a part of the star's contract, a kind of big perk for the "little people." When the film has two or even three big stars, they all may want to do it. Thus the multiplicity of producer credits.

When it comes to writers, though, the situation is different and more complicated. The Writers Guild of America allows only three writing credits on a feature film, although teams of two are credited as one, separated on the credits by an ampersand (you & I). However, if each of us works independently on the script (the most common system), we are separated by an "*and*" and credited as "you and I." But wait; you wrote the story on which the script is based, so you get "story by" credit, and your credit for the story precedes mine, even if I wrote most of the script, except that if my script made substantial changes to your story, I'll get first "screenplay by" credit. If more than two of us worked on the screenplay, the credits will probably read something like "screenplay by you & I and he and she." You and I worked as a team, but he and she worked separately. It actually does have a certain good logic to it, when you think about it. After all, the movie of *The Flintstones* had by various counts at least 35 and possibly as many as 60 writers who worked on the script. Somehow the system found a way to not list most of them, and for that we can be grateful.

The Directors Guild of America permits a film to list only one director, even when it is known that two or more worked on it. Except in very rare cases (a death in mid-production, and it had better be in the very middle of mid-production) there is only one directing credit. This is very good for a director's ego, certainly for the one who gets credit, but also for the one who doesn't, particularly if he or she had started production and then been removed by the producer at the insistence of the star or the studio. The public will not know that the removed one either screwed up or incurred the wrath of those more powerful. In either case, the removed one will live to direct another day. More rarely, a director will take the initiative and leave a production because of conflicts that cannot be resolved, again usually with the studio or the star. All of this will most likely take place either before or during the first few days of shooting.

We're not quite done yet. You may at some point have noticed the name George Spelvin, or Georgina Spelvin, or G. Spelvina or the like, among the acting credits on a film. That's traditionally the alias used by actors who for one reason or another do not want to be credited with their own names. There can be lots of reasons, ranging from unhappiness with the way the production turned out, to conflicts with the director or producer, or simply as an in joke. In the same way, directors have sometimes used "Alan Smithee" as their alias when they didn't want to be credited under their real name. In 1997 somebody even had the bright/stupid idea of making a real movie called *An Alan Smithee Film*. Not only did it bomb at the box office, but the real director took his name off the credits, so it really was an "Alan Smithee" film.

Now to the other end. When the movie fades to black, the end credits come up. Sometimes the first credits we see will go to the production crew, the people who worked on the shooting, and sometimes they will be for the cast, often in order of prominence in the film, though sometimes in order of appearance or in alphabetical order. The production crew credits will be where all the funny titles start coming up, and here's what they do. The gaffer is the chief electrician. He or she works for the director of photography, setting up all the lights as they are needed for shooting, directing a crew of other electricians, preparing the basic lighting for the next scenes to be shot, ordering all lighting equipment and supplies, and so forth. And guess who his or her top assistant is? Yes, the Best Boy. Sexist but accurate, at least until more women work their way into top crew positions.

Grips are the crew members who carry and set up equipment around the set or location. On most productions the head grip will be called the key grip, and on *very* big productions, where two crews will be shooting at the same time, there will be more than one key grip. The camera crew has its own grip, the dolly grip, who sets the camera up and then pushes the camera on its dolly or tracks, and there are grips who specialize in operating the camera crane when that is called for. Other grips will work with the carpenters to get and place the materials needed to assemble the sets. When the gaffer calls for particular lighting equipment it's the grips who will bring it and set it in place for the electricians to light and focus. Sometimes key grips are called best boys too, which can also make for confusion. A wrangler handles the animals, as you might expect, but there's no size limit. The film business has room for mouse, marmot, and cockroach wranglers as well. The greensman or woman is responsible for preparing and maintaining the live or fake flowers, foliage, trees, cornfields, or wastelands that you might see in the film.

Don't mistake odd titles for lack of skill. These are lifelong professionals who do extremely difficult jobs quickly and with very few mistakes; millions of dollars — and sometimes the safety of actors and other crew members — ride on how well they work. They apprentice for years before they get to take responsibility for a sizable production.

The director too has assistants, starting with, duh, the assistant director. The assistant director reports to the director, but he or she is more like an assistant producer. Assistant directors don't get to do much if any directing; they're more on a track toward production manager or producer. They break down the script, scene by scene, according to location or set or actors' calls (that is, what actors will be needed for shooting the scene). Then they put together a shooting schedule in the most efficient possible way, so as to get the most done in the least possible time with the most efficient use of people and equipment. A good A.D. can save a production hundreds of thousands of dollars just by analyzing the script and finding the best way to schedule how it should be shot. It's an incredibly demanding job, and because it relies so much on good communication between director and assistant, most directors will try to book their favorite assistants as much as possible.

Then there's the second assistant director, who's responsible for crew and cast calls, for keeping track of how many hours the crew has been on call so as to minimize overtime, sometimes for helping to cast extras when they're needed in a scene, and for working with cops and security to keep location shooting free from disturbances. And if you've noticed on big productions there are, yes, second second assistant directors, whose job as you might guess is to assist the second assistant director. Naturally, the second second assistant assistant assists the second second assistant, as if you didn't know.

When it comes to post-production, the titles proliferate. Most are self-explanatory, but you should know that a Foley artist is the person who — let me put it this way: In *Monty Python and the Holy Grail*, we see King Arthur riding his invisible horse around England. He is followed by his faithful retainer, who canters along behind him on foot, clapping two coconut shells together to make the clip-clop sound of a horse. The Foley artist is the person in the post-production studio who actually clopped the shells in front of a microphone to record the sound onto the film's sound track. He or she also makes the footsteps, the slide into third, the thud of a body slamming into a wall, and the like. The quintessential Foley-artist story comes from the Brian DePalma film *The Untouchables*, where we see Robert DeNiro as Al Capone whack somebody on the head with a baseball bat. So how do you create a sound to match the visual, and make it believable, without actually doing harm? After many experiments and many failures, the Foley artist found the right tools to record: a bowling pin hitting a raw turkey. You could try it yourself.

Almost all end credits, and the order in which they appear, have been settled for years by union contract and general industry convention. When there are massive amounts of special effects, as in the 1997 film *Titanic* or the 2000 film *The Perfect Storm*, the credits can run for what seems like hours. You and I are not expected to stay for them, but people in the business need to claim proper credit for whatever they did on a film, and end credits are the only way they can point to an acknowledgment of their work.

And now we come to the stars' credits, specifically the ones you see in newspaper ads. It is a world so difficult, so overloaded with the sight and sound of certain egos crashing toward oblivion while others ascend to heaven, that for a while in the 1980s it created a whole new cottage industry of movie ad credit designers. Let's start with what we may for the sake of argument call the good old days, which is anytime prior to 1970. For much of that time — certainly until the late 1950s — most actors were under contract to their studios, and it was the studio that decided who got top billing, who was billed above the title, and so on. When the studio system collapsed, it was only natural for actors and their agents to fight for billing, on a film by film basis; and by the 1970s most stars were writing into their picture contracts a description of how they were to be billed.

This was not a problem as long as only a few stars had the power to control the billing for any particular film. Perhaps your name was the only one with glitter enough to go above the title, though if my name was also a draw it was pretty easy to advertise us as you and I (above the title) in (the film's name here). But then, in the 1980s, things got complicated. Stars began to write into their contracts that their name had to be advertised, above the title, in letters no smaller than those of the film's title. Well, okay, that could be handled. But what if each of us had the same clause in our contract? And what if our names had more than, say, two letters, which has been known to happen? What if, say, our names were Harrison Ford, Renée Zellweger, and Leonardo DiCaprio? Could they all fit on one line in the ad? And each be the same height as the letters in the film's title? Not unless the film's title was as long as, say, *The Unbearable Lightness of Film Credit Machinations*, and the distributor bought six consecutive pages in the paper to advertise it.

So here's where the new designers came in. They found a way to make type faces so skinny, but with letters so tall, that they could fit the very longest names into a space no larger than a studio accountant's heart. Which is why you have such a hard time reading ads that give us more than one or two names above the title. The ad looks like this:

SKINNY STAR A   SKINNY STAR B   SKINNY STAR C
in
THE FILM

But wait; we're not quite done. Some stars require that their names be listed first, no matter who else is in the film. Okay, if nobody else is in the film. But what if two stars with equal power (or worse, even three or four) are in the same film with the same clause in their contracts? Are you beginning to see where this is going? We're not in gridlock yet, though, because some bright person came up with another solution. Give star A the first billing in the ads, but give star B a higher position. The ad then looks like this:

STAR B

STAR A

in

THE FILM

There are still more variations on the theme, such as clauses that require both first and highest billing in the ads, but obviously if the actors are serious about working on the film some accommodations will be reached, perhaps with additional money or perks, or even a quid pro quo for the next film, and everybody will accept the deal. So now you know.

CHAPTER 11

THE GREATEST FILM

What do we mean by great?

Well. Try looking up "great" in the dictionary. The definitions cover everything from dogs (Great Pyrenees) to relatives (great-grandmothers) to aristocrats (great ladies) to war (great bloodshed) to social life (we had a great time at your party). Fortunately we also get some descriptions that can work for movies: "Eminent, distinguished, markedly superior in character or quality, remarkably skilled." Not all that much to go on, but you sort of get the idea. "Great" is more an accumulation of adjectives than anything else, but it gives us a way to look at art — any art — and judge it.

All works of art start out with a really wide range of adjectives that people apply to them. The Impressionists, when they first showed, were denounced by some as horrible painters, loved by others as taking painting to a new level. The same range of reactions applied to the Cubists and Abstract Expressionists. But over time, the range of responses narrowed, and the negative comments dropped by the wayside. There came to be a consensus of opinion as to the worth of the paintings, and it was ultimately agreed that the best of them, and the best of the painters, should be called great. Not by papal dictum but by an informal, even unspoken agreement among those who happen to care about such things — practitioners, critics, scholars — supported by a long-term enthusiasm for the works among a lay audience of museum and gallery goers. Does that *really* make them great? Yes, for our purposes it does really make them great. Why else have the word in our language?

We use greatness as a measure of quality and value. But let's remember that the battle of the Cubists was fought almost a hundred years ago, and as in all arts, time is the judge. After three thousand years we still love the *Iliad*. That alone gives it greatness. After 500 years we still love the Sistine Chapel. After 400 years we still love *Romeo and Juliet*. After 200 years we still love *The Magic Flute*. But can we ask time to judge an art form that's only a hundred years old?

Maybe we can. Did London theatregoers know that Shakespeare would be judged greater than Jonson or Marlowe, or a dozen other playwrights on the boards at the time? Did they care? Sure they cared, and my guess is that a lot of them knew very well which plays were greater and which were lesser. How did they know? The same way you and I know — or think we know — which novels, plays, pieces of music, artworks, and, yes, movies will hold up. So let's not be afraid to try labeling films great, near-great, or just really good; and if time doesn't bear us out we'll be long past caring anyway.

One last point about greatness in a film. Harry Cohn, the legendary founder and head of Columbia Pictures, had a surefire test about whether a film was going to make money. He said that his ass could always tell if a film was going to be good or if it would bomb. He screened all his pictures, and if he squirmed in his seat the film was no good. If he didn't, then the film would make money. "If I'm bored, they're bored," he said about the audience. My test is a little different, though maybe not all that much. If you and your best friend find that you absolutely have to talk about a certain movie at least ten times, on ten different occasions after you've seen it, then it's likely to have greatness. Nine or fewer, and it's never going to make it.

Does it take a great filmmaker to make a great film?

Back in September of 1947, in the sixth game of the World Series, a role player for the Brooklyn Dodgers named Al Gionfriddo ran back to the bullpen in left field at Yankee Stadium and robbed Joe Dimaggio of a home run that would have won the game and the series for the Yankees. It was a great play. The question is, was Gionfriddo a great player? The answer is no. He was up in the majors for just four years, couldn't hit, and in fact was gone the next year. In May of 1997 a bench player for the Phoenix Suns named Rex Chapman, who'd been bouncing around the NBA for nine years, came through in the playoffs with a league record nine 3-point baskets in one game against the Seattle Sonics; then, in the next game, with one second left and the Suns down by three, he got an inbounds pass thirty-five feet out, turned, leaped, and threw a one-handed shot that got nothing but net to tie the game and send it into overtime. Was it a great shot? Yes. Was Chapman a great player? No, because he couldn't do it game after game, year after year. He did it once, and maybe that was enough for a footnote in the recorded history of basketball, but he didn't come close to greatness.

Was Michael Jordan a great player? Yes, of course. Why? Because game after game, year after year, he did great things on the basketball court. Was he great at *all* things on the court? No. He wasn't a great post-up center. He wasn't a great play maker. But he didn't have to be great at all things to be great. Magic Johnson was a genius at reading defenses, making plays, and shooting anywhere from the foul line in. And he was a great player, with a great career over many years. One or two (or three or four) great plays don't make a great player, though they're not a bad start. It takes all the virtues that your parents tried to instill in you: hard work, consistency, and talent, though it helps to be a genius.

Unlike a great catch or a great shot in sports, but like any work of art, movies aren't made in an instant. They don't spring whole from the brow of the artist. In 1941 Orson Welles made *Citizen Kane*. It was his first film, and a great film, and if he had never made another one we would still regard it as great. But it didn't come out of nowhere. Welles had directed, written, and acted in many theatre productions and radio plays for five years before. They were innovative, brilliant, and powerful. And when he went to Hollywood he brought that talent — more than talent, that genius — with him. And he brought a troupe of actors who trusted him and whom he trusted, because they had worked together on a whole range of pieces. Herman Mankiewicz delivered a bold and fascinating screenplay based on the life of William Randolph Hearst. And when the movie was released, it was a stunning success. For almost sixty years it's stayed on almost everyone's list as one of the greatest films ever made.

The downside of genius, in Welles's case, is that Hearst hated it, and as the most powerful media owner in the United States he decided to use that power to break Welles. Which he did. So the moral of the story is that the success of *Citizen Kane* both made and destroyed Welles's career. He never again got either the money or the support he wanted, for any film, from any studio, for the rest of his life. But there is enough greatness in each of his successive films, flawed though they are, to bear out the judgment that he was a great filmmaker.

Just as in sports, there are artists in every art form whose lifetime of work varies from mediocre to very good, say, and yet somehow one piece, one painting, one work will be sublime, a work for the ages. In classical music, for example, Leoncavallo produced *Pagliacci* in the course of a lifetime of ordinary work. Englebert Humperdinck (the original) managed to come up with *Hansel & Gretel*. Carl Orff wrote *Carmina Burana*. These are artists' versions of the Al Gionfriddo-Rex Chapman plays, because even you or I might once in a lifetime make a basket like Chapman or a catch like Gionfriddo. But unlike them we never played in the big leagues, never wrote operas or oratorios, and in a lifetime we could never make any of these pieces unless we had worked for years at our craft, as they did.

So the answer to the question, does it take a great filmmaker to make a great film, is that it takes at least a very good filmmaker to make a great film, and it helps to be great. But we should remember that some very good filmmakers make only very good films, rather than great ones, just as some very good novelists never achieve greatness. We can put Robert Altman, Martin Scorsese, and John Sayles in that group of very good filmmakers. Obviously there's nothing wrong with making very good films. We're lucky to have them in our lives. But it's the difference between Magic Johnson and James Worthy, on the old Lakers team. Worthy was a very good ballplayer who consistently played at the upper limit of his talent because he had Magic to feed him. He had great moments, but not greatness. A very good filmmaker can become a great filmmaker, but we should see at least the hint of greatness in every film he or she makes.

So what's the definition of a great filmmaker? First, there has to be a substantial body of work that is "eminent, distinguished, markedly superior in character or quality, remarkably skilled." Next, the artist's work has to resonate within us, the audience. It can't be so hermetic that only the filmmaker gets it. It can't be trite, or derivative, or pompous. It can't reveal everything it has to say in just one viewing. The great artist's work has the ability to slip through our defenses and our social facade, to show us something about our lives that we may have hidden from ourselves or others. And there has to be enough in it that we can come back to it again and again, with pleasure and passion.

Third and last, it has to have that elusive quality known as "artistry" — sometimes seen as technical command, or simply the coherence of every facet of the work — so that the writing, the direction, the acting, the photography and lighting and editing, are all making some kind of positive contribution to the filmmaker's vision. Those are tough criteria, but we're talking about a pantheon here, a hall of fame. If you let everybody in you just demean the award.

Naming names: some great filmmakers and what they've done

I have a list of great filmmakers. Each of them has made at least one great feature film in the sound era, *and* the signs of greatness are hanging around in their other films as well. I arbitrarily distinguish between filmmakers whose films are simply wonderful and those that are great. So you won't see Alfred Hitchcock here, or Sergio Leone, or John Huston, or Howard Hawks or John Ford or Frank Capra either, for that matter. They're wonderful but they're not great. You *will* find them in Chapter 12, though, so don't lose hope. Maybe you'll notice that a couple of icons of the sixties — which really was an Elizabethan age of film, a decade in which dozens of filmmakers churned out scores of breathtaking films — are missing too. I call them the formerly great. Into that bin I hesitantly put Fellini, Antonioni, Jean-Luc Godard, Stanley Kubrick, and Alain Resnais. Their day may well come again, and I might be among the first to welcome them, but not yet.

My list is surprisingly short, but it's my best guess as to whose statues I would order for the pantheon. What you will see are some people you know and some you may never have heard of. They are, in alphabetical order, Ingmar Bergman, Robert Bresson, Luis Buñuel, Francis Ford Coppola, Vittorio De Sica, Rainer Werner Fassbinder, Akira Kurosawa, Louis Malle, Kenji Mizoguchi, Satyajit Ray, François Truffaut, and Orson Welles.

Ingmar Bergman

If the fifties and sixties were the Elizabethan age of film, Bergman is as close as we ever got to Shakespeare. Not a poet, and almost without a sense of humor, Bergman managed in nearly forty films to illuminate more facets of our lives, more deeply, than anyone who ever worked in film. He dealt with marriages, with family relationships, with war and cowardice, with whether life has any ultimate meaning, and if so just what that might be, and with religion. His masterpieces include *The Seventh Seal*, *Persona*, *Cries and Whispers*, and *Scenes From a Marriage*. But don't forget to see his filmed version of *The Magic Flute* as well.

Robert Bresson

The French writer-director Bresson is almost forgotten today. He worked from the 1940s to the early 1970s, and always had problems getting enough financing for his films. They are austere in their structure, and yet there's a sensuous undercurrent that runs through them. Perhaps his most famous film is *A Man Escaped*, about a French agent taken prisoner by the Germans in World War II, who plans an "impossible" escape. But for me, the three Bresson films that put him in the pantheon are *Mouchette*, about a young farm girl and her encounters with love and death; *The Trial of Joan of Arc*; and *Une Femme Douce*, with Dominique Sanda as the protagonist of a disastrous love affair, in a story taken from Dostoyevsky.

Luis Buñuel

In a way, Buñuel is the most fun of any of the greats. His movies are filled with strange and witty dislocations of time and place and perspective. He's always asking us to think about what's real and what's just our fantasy, and he'll blithely switch from one to the other without telling us, and then expect us to follow along. But that doesn't mean he's shallow or superficial. He made films from 1930 to 1977, in Spain, France, Mexico, and the United States. You might want to see *Los Olvidados*, about young slum boys in Mexico City, and his version, the best ever, of *Robinson Crusoe*. He reached his peak with two breathtaking French films: *Belle de Jour*, with Catherine Deneuve as a housewife who works as a prostitute during the day; and *The Discreet Charm of the Bourgeoisie*, about a group of wealthy layabouts whose dinner party is always being interrupted, usually by things like war and death.

Francis Ford Coppola

Coppola is here because *The Godfather* (Part I) is without question the most perfect feature film ever made, and because *The Godfather Part II* is almost as good. In spite of Coppola's later comments that making *The Godfather* was a very painful experience and filled with conflict in every area of production, the film remains miraculously powerful and coherent, with Brando and Pacino leading more than a dozen major actors in a piece of ensemble work that's never been matched. We'll talk some more about this later in the chapter.

Vittorio De Sica

Another director nearly forgotten these days, De Sica made four shattering films about the aftermath of war — *Shoeshine, The Bicycle Thief, Umberto D* and *Two Women* — and then went on to make a few of the best comedies, including *Miracle in Milan* and *The Gold of Naples*. But he wasn't quite through, because at the end of his life he made *The Garden of the Finzi-*

Continis, a breathtaking film that dealt with an old Italian-Jewish family trying not to confront the reality of World War II.

Rainer Werner Fassbinder

Fassbinder was the bad boy of film in the seventies and eighties, but before he died of a cocaine overdose he managed to make a group of films that, how shall I say this, boldly went where no man (or woman) had dared to go before. Probably the best of them is *The Marriage of Maria Braun*, which is an allegory of Germany's rise to power after the second World War, told through the life of a war widow who manages to survive and triumph over death, poverty, blight, and corruption. Fascinating and moving from the first frame to the last, this is a work that owes little to anyone and any tradition but the one that Fassbinder created out of his own talent.

Akira Kurosawa

Kurosawa is the master whom everyone copies and the best ones learn from. He's adapted Shakespeare (*King Lear* into *Ran*, *Macbeth* into *Throne of Blood*) and Gorky (*The Lower Depths*), and even an Ed McBain detective story (*High and Low*). His *The Seven Samurai* was remade into an American classic, *The Magnificent Seven*. You can look at any Kurosawa film and you won't find a wasted moment or a bad shot composition. And as wonderful as his earlier films are, he transcended them all with *Ran*, his last full production, which is more a meditation on *Lear* by an artist of genius, rather than simply an adaptation.

Louis Malle

Art-house addicts have known Malle for more than forty years of moviemaking that defies genres. He's made comedies like *Murmur of the Heart*, *The Lovers*, *Viva Maria*, and *Zazie dans le Metro*. He's made exquisitely powerful films about the underside of war, like *Lacombe, Lucien*, and *Au Revoir les Enfants*. In the United States, he's made *Pretty Baby*, *Atlantic City*, *My Dinner With André*, and *Vanya on 42nd Street*. And back in the sixties he also made an amazing 6-part documentary on India that is so powerful it is still not permitted to be shown there. His films are so accessible they're often taken too lightly. Don't underestimate him.

Kenji Mizoguchi

Mizogŭchi — almost unknown in the United States — was through the 1930s the John Ford of Japan, making costume dramas and contemporary-life films by the dozens. He belongs here by virtue of three films he made in the 1950s, at the end of his career: *Sansho the Bailiff*, *Ugetsu*, and *The Life of Oharu*. *Sansho*, about a petty tyrant in medieval Japan and the people who are his victims, is the most profound examination of evil, and what it means to resist evil, ever shown on film. Both *Ugetsu* and *Oharu* are more relaxed, more breathable if you like, and yet they too are gems.

Satyajit Ray

The pain, the terror, the sorrow, and the gorgeous exhilaration of Indian life are part of every film Ray made. His so-called *Apu* trilogy, made early in his career, is about a family caught between the security of tradition and the demands of contemporary life. It touches everyone who sees it because Ray makes us confront the universal elements that are overtones to any one family's story. All his films have wit and beauty that exist side by side with the pain. Ray was a natural filmmaker; that is, he had the ability to compose, shoot, and edit everything he did so perfectly that we are never jarred or misled or confused by anything in his work. Every shot just seems to add to our understanding. A rare gift.

François Truffaut

Another genius with a camera, Truffaut made films about making films (*Day for Night*), about children coming to terms with an adult world (*The 400 Blows*, *The Wild Child*, *Small Change*), about adults who act like children (*Shoot the Piano Player* and the Antoine Doinel films), and one absolutely supreme masterpiece, *Jules and Jim*, that brings everything together in just 100 minutes of screen time. This story of two men and their love for one woman (played by Jeanne Moreau) over more than two decades, from the years before World War I to the coming of the Nazis, is without question the greatest romance ever put on film.

Orson Welles

No one knows what Orson Welles might have done had the studios not cut him off at the knees. Film students tend to think of *Citizen Kane* as old news, because every device and technique in it is so familiar. But nobody had ever made a movie like it before, and everyone has stolen from it since. For many years a consensus of film critics has called it the greatest film ever made, though if it has a flaw it comes in treating its characters analytically rather than empathically. Still, not to be missed. Welles followed it with *The Magnificent Ambersons*, from a Booth Tarkington novel, which although cut by the studio and even reshot in parts, has the brilliance of *Kane* with an added depth of characterization missing from the first film.

THE GREATEST FILM EVER MADE

The Godfather (Part I, 1972) — Picture yourself watching this movie for the first time, on the night it opened, back in 1972. Maybe you read Mario Puzo's book, most likely you didn't. So you don't know very much about what you're going to see. And what will you see?

Marlon Brando hears from a petitioner in *The Godfather (Part I)*.

Well, you won't see a whodunit, or a mystery, or a crime and punishment film. There isn't a cops-and-robbers chase anywhere in it. There isn't even a hero, much less a superhero. The closest we come is the Godfather himself, played by Marlon Brando, and he's the head of one of New York's five Mafia families, who makes his money from prostitution, gambling, and extortion and doesn't have a moment's regret about it.

Maybe you could say his son Michael, played by Al Pacino, is a hero, since he's brilliant and dedicated to the success of the family. But most heroes have some moral compass in them, and you would have a hard time finding one in Michael. A critic would call him a picaresque hero, meaning you like him, maybe even love him, but he's a bastard.

So what is it that makes this the greatest film of all time? Three things:

1. The characters are brilliantly drawn. They're real, they're fascinating, they're unpredictable yet always true to their nature.
2. The plot is built on the interplay of those very natures, one against another, just as real life is. We in the audience can come back again and again, even though we know what's going to happen, because we see so much of ourselves and our own lives in what's on the screen. It's what happens with any great work of art. We may know every note of Handel's "Messiah," but that doesn't keep us from wanting to hear it again and again.
3. The elements of the film itself: Coppola's direction, the dialogue by Coppola and Puzo, Gordon Willis's photography and lighting, Nino Rota's music, and the acting by a group who fit themselves to their roles instead of the other way around. The film is long — almost three hours — and has not even one wasted moment in it. There's not an unnecessary scene, not one bad line of dialogue. Take even a minute away and *The Godfather* would be lessened.

Let's look at Coppola's direction. His actors live their roles as people, not "characters." We don't see Al Pacino as Michael. We see Michael. We don't see James Caan as Sonny. We see Sonny. And of course Brando as Don Vito Corleone has become the most imitated character in film history. He is larger than life, a figure who dominates just by virtue of living, and yet is completely human and without pretension.

Interestingly, in Brando's autobiography he demeans Coppola, telling us that he, Brando, didn't pay much attention to what Coppola said, and didn't even bother to memorize his lines, relying on cue cards and notes pinned to other actors' clothing. In the end it doesn't matter, and maybe Coppola let him do it because he knew how great the performance was, and didn't want to interfere. If so, it was a brilliant decision, because the film's genius lies in letting us see into each of these people without even the hint of a stereotype. Coppola builds all of the film's actions out of the personalities he and Puzo have given each of them. There are no coincidences, no contrived moments of revelation or reconciliation. We *know* these people. We know their needs, their fears, their secrets, and their fantasies, as well as we know our own families and friends. Perfection.

Then, there's the script. It is a model for any screenwriting class. In the very opening sequence — starting with the opening shot itself — we grasp the nature of the story, the character and personality of everyone in it, the relative power each has, and the upcoming plot developments. Here's how it starts: The screen is black, and we hear Nino Rota's haunting theme music. Then we hear a voice, in an Italian accent, say, "I believe in America." We fade in on a closeup of a middle-aged man with a mustache talking about how he came to America to make a good life here, and how his beautiful daughter was beaten by her boyfriend so that she is now ugly. As he tells his story the shot widens slowly and we see in the foreground the hand of another man. We are in the home and office of the Godfather, and this speaker is a supplicant who wants help from the Godfather to kill the young man, who was given only a suspended sentence by the court.

This is all the opening shot of the film, slowly widening out, and so far all we've seen is the Godfather's hand, in the foreground, with fingers resting against the side of his head. As the man goes deeper into his story, he breaks down, and the hand makes a little gesture. Immediately someone brings the supplicant a glass of brandy to help him. The shot finally widens enough to show us the whole room, and the Godfather's men standing by. We have learned everything we need to know about the Godfather, about what he does and how he does it, and why. All in one shot.

And in the next five minutes we learn that it is the Godfather's daughter's wedding day, we meet his sons, we learn more about his business, and the film is off and running. It has been called the greatest opening sequence in film history, and I would agree. The film never lets us down. In its characterizations of the family and its friends and enemies, people bring their own success or destruction upon themselves because of their own natures. Sonny, the heir apparent, is a hothead. He both succeeds and fails because of it. Michael is brilliant and calculating but without a conscience, and there will be a heavy price to pay for his decisions.

There's an abundance of plot, and yet when we've seen the film once we're not satisfied that we've seen it all. We know everything that will happen, but as with any great work of art we want to come back again and again, to see it again, to hear the lines again, to live again with the people who inhabit it. We begin to notice the shots, the lighting, the music. We see how characters in the background come forward for their moment or their scene, and how those moments enrich everything else in the film.

And there are the astounding visuals: The most notorious image, of course, is the shot of Woltz, the Hollywood producer, waking up to find the horse's head under the covers with him. But there is also Sonny stopping at the toll booth, the explosion in Sicily, the betrayal at Vito Corleone's funeral, the death of Luca Brazzi. And at the end, the cross-cutting between the baptism of Connie's son and the executions of Michael's enemies.

None of these moments or images is dropped in gratuitously, for the sake of adding excitement to a flagging story line. They all grow out of the personalities and the conflicts that beset the Corleone family, and odd as it may sound, the Corleones are more like you and me than we would ever want to admit to ourselves. That's the greatness, and the genius, of *The Godfather*.

CHAPTER 12

A LIST OF ALL THE FILMS YOU HAVE TO SEE BEFORE YOU DIE

We all need structure in our lives, so let me do you the favor of identifying every film you really have to see, because you never know how much more you'll be able to cram into your life. Seize the day, or at least the film. Also, I'm not interested in making you a better person. That's why you won't find *Gandhi* on the list. On the other hand, you will find *Malcolm X*, in spite of its hackneyed opening section and midpoint bogus conversion, because that film has much more kinetic interest than *Gandhi*, and not necessarily because of its political viewpoint.

One thing this list is not is my ordering of the greatest films of all time. Not only would my list be different from anybody else's, but there are some widely accepted "greatest" films that you don't have to see at all if you don't want to. One of them is Jean Renoir's *The Rules of the Game*, which is also not on the list. It's a great film, but every time I teach it or screen it for normal people, as opposed to students of film, it gets absolutely no reaction at all. It's the kind of film that takes a graduate degree to appreciate, or at least some directing credits. Don't bother unless you have one or the other.

On the other hand, there are a lot of films on the list that definitely aren't great at all, but you still absolutely have to see them. *Clueless, Top Secret!*, and the Errol Flynn *Adventures of Robin Hood* come to mind. I particularly like *Top Secret!* for the moment when the good scientist imprisoned in the dungeon says that the wicked East Germans plan to test his powerful new magnet on Sunday. "Hmmm," says Val Kilmer, "and that's Simchas Torah."

I've been somewhat unfair, even arbitrary, about categorizing the films. All the "foreign" films are lumped together, no matter what their content or style, or even their country of origin or filmmaker, while I've carefully separated the English-language films into lots of groups. I apologize, but I really don't know of a better way.

One last word: Don't start at the top and work your way down the list. Start with what appeals to you, what jumps out at you, what sounds like fun. Then pick and choose till you're either terminally bored, or dead, or both. That's a good place to stop.

MUSICALS

The list is small and eclectic, but if you've seen these six everything else is just more of the same.

Singin' in the Rain — (1952, directed by Gene Kelly and Stanley Donen) Would you believe that this film was originally designed to star Howard Keel? What would they have done for the dances? "I'm stumblin', I'm shufflin' in the rain." Think of this as the miracle that almost wasn't. You'll love it for every reason mentioned in Chapter 7, plus the exquisite pleasure of seeing Donald O'Connor at the top of his form.

The Commitments — (1991, directed by Alan Parker) So realistic it plays like a documentary, and yet there is not even one moment when Parker loses control. Gorgeous R&B music, arranged, sung, and played to perfection by a cast of amateurs and semi-professionals with great wit and verve. It is full of brilliant lines and honest, powerful moments that give it a depth beyond any other film with music that I know.

Top Hat — (1935, directed by Mark Sandrich) Sit back, relax, and enjoy. Astaire and Rogers, the two greatest popular dancers of the century, sing and dance their way through a silky-smooth, charming Irving Berlin score. This is the best of their musicals, and a pleasure from beginning to end.

Yankee Doodle Dandy — (1942, directed by Michael Curtiz) It's hard to remember that the songwriter/entertainer George M. Cohan was once an American icon. James Cagney, who had gotten typecast as a heavy, shows here what a brilliant song-and-dance man he was. He won a well-deserved Oscar for his performance.

Cabaret — (1972, directed by Bob Fosse) An exciting production of the Broadway musical by Kander and Ebb about young Sally Bowles, the innocent singer caught in the oncoming madness of 1930s Berlin. Liza Minelli and Joel Grey both won Oscars, as did Fosse and the film itself. A most unusual film that doesn't shy away from the frightening political implications.

A Hard Day's Night — (1964, directed by Richard Lester) Lester used a hand-held camera and lots of jump cuts to capture the wit and charm of the early Beatles. If the technique seems dated today it's just because everybody's copied it since then. You'll see why millions fainted in ecstasy at the fab four.

COMEDIES

Comedy should be healing, and I'm not sure *Annie Hall* belongs on the list, since it's basically an autobiographical drama told with wit, so it's okay with me if you want to move it to another category. On the other hand, a number of people tell me that they watch it at least once a year, which has to put it into the healing category, at least for them. Of course, I wonder about people like that, but I guarantee that any or all of the other films here will heal anything that ails you.

Some of you will notice that there's no Marx Brothers film included. I've waited years to omit them. There are funny moments and a few wisecracks here and there, but take my advice and watch *Million Dollar Legs* instead.

City Lights — (1931, directed by Charles Chaplin) Hilarious comic setpieces alternate with unspeakably maudlin tearjerking, as Chaplin's tramp gets involved with both a drunken millionaire and a blind flower-seller who needs an operation to restore her sight. Not my favorite, but there are a couple of exquisitely funny scenes. And Pauline Kael called the closing scene the "greatest moment in films." You decide.

Modern Times — (1936, directed by Charles Chaplin) The best and purest Chaplin since the early two-reelers. He foregoes the pathos here, and works with the young Paulette Goddard to give us a film that — well into the sound era — is the apotheosis of silent comedy. The opening sequence in the factory, and the roller skating in the department store, are exquisite.

The General — (1927, directed by Buster Keaton) Keaton made much more richly textured films than Chaplin, and this one rewards us with everything from breathtaking slapstick to Mathew Brady-style photography. It's a graduate level course in silent comedy, in just 80 minutes of screen time.

The Court Jester — (1956, directed by Norman Panama and Melvin Frank) A miracle of writing, direction, casting and acting, with enough goings-on at the castle to fill a dozen films. Danny Kaye gives us the two funniest sequences since the introduction of sound: the wine merchant stopped on the road, and the vessel with the pestle. Basil Rathbone is the villain, of course, and Angela Lansbury, in her first comic role, shows great timing. If you chose this as your very last film, you'd die happy.

Monty Python and the Holy Grail — (1975, directed by Terry Gilliam and Terry Jones) The genius of Monty Python was that they played everything straight and let the comedy take care of itself. From the early moments of "Bring out your dead" and the anarcho-syndicalist collective to the problem of facing the attack bunny to the infamous three questions at the climax, this is the group's most perfectly realized film.[3]

Annie Hall — (1977, directed by Woody Allen) I'm in the minority here. "Annie Hall" has its moments, but not very many of them. I do like the Cheder boy's visit to Grammy Hall in Wisconsin, but the story is so thin and the gags so few and far between, that whatever impact it might have had is quickly lost. Don't look for it in the next edition. (Do I hear you say "Don't worry, there won't be a next edition?")

Sleeper — (1973, directed by Woody Allen) On the other hand, this is Allen's most consistently funny film, with a fine premise (he wakes up 200 years from now into a totalitarian world), lots of sex (in the Orgasmatron), and a hundred or more of his best gags and lines, including some very prescient ones about cloning human beings.

The Lady Eve — (1941, directed by Preston Sturges) Preston Sturges is an acquired taste, and not for everyone, but with a good script that gives card sharp/con woman Barbara Stanwyck the chance to show what a fine comedian she was, and Mr. Sincerity Henry Fonda as her foil, this is a lot of fun.

The Princess Bride — (1987, directed by Rob Reiner) Written by William Goldman for his kids, this is one of the few films that works for both

---

[3] In the early 1970s, when the troupe was at the height of its popularity, the German government invited them to Bavaria, to combine a tour with a vacation. They landed at Munich and asked to visit the notorious concentration camp at Dachau, just a few miles outside the city. No one seemed to know where it was. "I've never seen it." "I know nothing." They drove around all day, and finally got to the entrance late in the afternoon, but it was closed for the day and they were told they couldn't come in. "Tell them we're Jewish," said Graham Chapman.

children and adults. Mandy Patinkin and Billy Crystal keep things humming, with Fred Savage and Peter Falk bookending the story. Maybe I'm prejudiced, but we brought our kids up on this one and they turned out all right. I still cry at Falk's last line.

Million Dollar Legs — (1932, directed by Edward Cline) Cline had codirected some of Buster Keaton's films, and used that experience here to pull together a story that gives us W.C. Fields as the president of Klopstockia trying to make money for his country by having his presidential messenger, who runs faster than a speeding bullet, enter the 1932 Olympics in Los Angeles. Ben Turpin, the silent film comedian, is the speed demon. Jack Oakie is Sweetheart, an American vacuum cleaner salesman who falls in love with the president's daughter.

Clueless — (1995, directed by Amy Heckerling) The achievement was to take a purely English novel — *Emma* — and convert it into a profile of quintessentially American teens, with warmth and love. You think you know your own kids? As if! It moves fast, so pick up on the boys' fashion sense, the driving test, the nose bandages, and the ubiquitous cell phones.

His Girl Friday — (1940, directed by Howard Hawks) This remake of *The Front Page* adds a lot by making the star reporter female (Rosalind Russell) formerly married to her editor (Cary Grant). It's faster and funnier this way, with slamming doors, hidden murder suspects in a newsroom rolltop desk, and an earnest fiancé (Ralph Bellamy) bumbling around the edges of the plot.

M*A*S*H — (1970, directed by Robert Altman) Altman's most perfect film gives Donald Sutherland and Elliott Gould enough play room to demolish every convention of military life and then some, and they don't let us down. They're one of the great comedy pairs in film history. Forget the now-dated sexist moments; this film just gets better and better the more times you see it.

Top Secret! — (1984, directed by Jim Abrahams, David Zucker, Jerry Zucker) The most consistently funny of the trio's parodies, it's worth treasuring for the Swedish bookstore scene alone, but don't forget the Pinto and the tank, the cow and the bull, and Omar Sharif and the windshield wipers.

Hot Shots! — (1991, directed by Jim Abrahams) Charlie Sheen shows marvelous deadpan wit in this parody of *Top Gun* and about a dozen other hero films. There's a great gag under the opening credits, on the deck of an aircraft carrier, and see if you can spot the parade ground hora outside Admiral Lloyd Bridges' window.

Airplane! — (1980, directed by Jim Abrahams, David Zucker, Jerry Zucker) The first of the group's big films, it gave us the singing nun who cuts off the little girl's oxygen, plus Tommy in the cockpit with Peter Graves, the south sea island barroom brawl and dance, and the strangest-sounding jetliner in history.

Ferris Bueller's Day Off — (1986, directed by John Hughes) Hughes's best film, this is the fulfillment of every adolescent's dream, where a guilt-free high school student wreaks havoc with the administration while treating himself and his friends to a great day in Chicago. You'll particularly like Matthew Broderick and the German Oompah band doing "Twist & Shout" down Michigan Avenue.

Twentieth Century — (1934, directed by Howard Hawks) Ben Hecht and Charles MacArthur wrote the script from their Broadway hit. John Barrymore as an egomaniacal Broadway producer shows what a great farceur he was, and Carole Lombard as his unwilling star matches him blow for blow. It all takes place on the old Twentieth Century Limited streamliner, and it's the very best comic film of the 1930s. No kidding.

FOREIGN FILMS

You'd do just fine if *all* you ever saw before you died was this group of foreign films. They're listed alphabetically, but they don't need to be seen in any particular order. Once you start, though, I know you'll stay the course. Don't be surprised to find yourself calling the mail-order catalog companies for more — and more — and more — by these filmmakers.

Babette's Feast — (1987, directed by Gabriel Axel) What Garrison Keillor has left out of his analyses of Lutheran angst this film completes. Exiled Parisienne Stephane Audran comes to a cold and dismal Danish village to work in the house of two bloodless sisters, but she cannot quite escape her sensuous talents, and so gives them an extraordinary gift. From an Isak Dinesen short story. In Danish.

Belle de Jour — (1967, directed by Luis Buñuel) Essence of Buñuel. Catherine Deneuve is an unsatisfied upper-middle-class wife who mixes fantasy and reality by working days in a whorehouse. Only Buñuel could make it play, and only Buñuel could make it funny. It takes a couple of viewings to decide which scenes are reality and which are fantasy. In French.

Breathless — (1959, directed by Jean-Luc Godard) This is the film that started the revolution. Hand-held camera, available lighting, jump cuts within scenes and within each shot as well. An incredibly kinetic experience at the time, it's not Godard's fault that it seems tame today. Jean-Paul Belmondo is a killer on the run, Jean Seberg is his girlfriend, sort of. In French and English.

Children of Paradise — (1945, directed by Marcel Carné). An unspeakably gushy fantasy of theatre life as a metaphor for real life. You don't really need to see it before you die, because they're probably playing it every day up in actors' heaven, where egos go to live forever. Included here only because everybody but me absolutely loves it. Is that a reason? In French.

The Conformist — (1971, directed by Bernardo Bertolucci) A knowing and unsparing work about sex and cowardice in fascist 1930s Italy, with Jean-Louis Trintignant as a man trying to choose between courage and expediency, and Dominique Sanda as a temptress. Bertolucci wrote the screenplay from the novel by Alberto Moravia, and Vittorio Storaro, who went on to photograph *Apocalypse Now* and *Reds*, among others, was the cinematographer. His camerawork and lighting will stun you with their beauty. In Italian and French.

Cries and Whispers — (1972, directed by Ingmar Bergman) A woman not yet 40 is dying of cancer, and she, her two sisters, and her servant woman must deal with a lifetime's worth of love, hate, and unasked and unanswered questions. Sven Nyqvist won an Oscar for his cinematography. In Swedish.

Cyrano de Bergerac — (1990, directed by Jean-Paul Rappeneau) Gérard Depardieu is the definitive Cyrano; his performance in this clichéd old romance is a work of genius. He gives us the best-ever versions of the great comic setpieces (the recitation of nose jokes), he makes Cyrano's legendary swordplay and strength believable, and if you aren't in tears at the end you have the heart of a grinch. Brilliantly subtitled for the French-language-impaired by Anthony Burgess. In French.

The Discreet Charm of the Bourgeoisie — (1972, directed by Luis Buñuel) A group of upscale layabouts keeps having its dinner parties interrupted by annoying things like war, robbery, and death. Is this a comedy? Of course. It's your best introduction to the mind and genius of Buñuel, who is well worth knowing for films that are unlike anybody else's. In French.

La Dolce Vita — (1960, directed by Federico Fellini) This is the film that made Marcello Mastroianni a star, and it has one of the great opening scenes of all time: a huge statue of Christ flying over the city of Rome, on its way to the Vatican. Mastroianni is a reporter for a *Star*-like tabloid that follows the

Gerard Depardieu silences a critic in *Cyrano de Bergerrac*.

rich and glamorous. The film's ironic title — "The Sweet Life" — lets Fellini explore issues of morality, courage, and cowardice. In Italian.

La Femme Infidèle — (1969, directed by Claude Chabrol) A simple, softly-spoken film, in which a wife has an affair and her lover is murdered. Chabrol is not interested in suspense, a la Hitchcock; his actors simply live out their lives in front of the camera, but the implications are enormous. Stéphane Audran (Chabrol's wife) gives an exquisitely nuanced performance as the unfaithful wife. In French.

Forbidden Games — (1951, directed by René Clément) A little French girl's parents are killed by strafing planes at the start of World War II. She's taken in by a peasant family, but cannot make sense of life and death, and so — with the complicity of the family's young son — she begins to create death and burial rituals of her own. An original and powerful look at the unforeseen ramifications of war. In French.

Grand Illusion — (1937, directed by Jean Renoir) Perhaps the greatest of all war films, it has barely a battle scene in it. Set for the most part in a World War I German prison camp for French and British prisoners, it gives us a glimpse of what it means to live the clichés of bravery and courage. Extraordinary performances by Erich von Stroheim, Jean Gabin, and Pierre Fresnay. In French, English, and German.

Ikiru (To Live) — (1952, directed by Akira Kurosawa) A middle-aged bureaucrat learns that he has only a few months to live, considers the little he's accomplished, and decides to do something meaningful in the time he has left. This is a thoughtful, fascinating story with obvious resonance for the rest of us. It's about as far from Kurosawa's samurai epics as it's possible to get. In Japanese.

Jean de Florette and *Manon of the Spring* — (1986, directed by Claude Berri) This amazing two-part epic is the story of a naive would-be farmer (Gérard Depardieu) in the dry hills of Provence who is tricked by a greedy neighbor (Yves Montand) and his nephew; and of the consequences to all of them, over two generations. It is so powerful, and leads to an ending so cathartic, that this simple country story has the resonance of a Greek tragedy. In French.

Ju Dou — (1989, directed by Zhang Yimou) Set in a village in 1920s China, this is the beautifully photographed, agonizing story of a frightful love triangle. A young peasant woman (Gong Li) is made to marry the elderly owner of a factory that dyes fabrics. She falls in love with his young nephew and must deal with her husband's revenge. In Mandarin.

Jules and Jim — (1962, directed by François Truffaut) A work of genius, where every creative element — writing, direction, acting, photography, editing, music — has illuminated Truffaut's vision and brought the film as close as a human being's creation can come to perfection. The story of a three-sided love affair that begins in Paris before World War I and lasts for almost thirty years, it encompasses comedy, romance, and tragedy in a way that no other film has ever done. It helps to see it on the big screen, but in any case it helps to see it. In French.

Lacombe, Lucien — (1974, directed by Louis Malle) A strange young country boy wants to join the French resistance during World War II, but instead becomes an informer for the Gestapo, at the same time falling in love with a Jewish girl. In this amazing film, Malle finds a way to show us the resonance that Lucien's story has for all our lives. In French.

M — (1931, directed by Fritz Lang) Peter Lorre was a cabaret comic in Berlin, but by day he played a psychopathic child murderer in this film. The people of the city demand action, so the police and the underworld find themselves joined in an uneasy alliance of parallel searches to identify the murderer so that crime and police work can both continue undisturbed. Lorre's performance is a miracle of tension and pity. In German.

The Marriage of Maria Braun — (1978, directed by Rainer Werner Fassbinder) This allegory of Germany's postwar rise is told through the life of Maria Braun, a war widow and a survivor, who finds a way to achieve prosperity and ultimately great wealth. Hanna Schygulla is Maria in this brutal, witty, insightful look at what makes the world go round. In German.

Les Miserables — (1995, directed by Claude Lelouch) Please note that this is not the novel. It's a reworking of the themes, as lived out through two generations in the twentieth century. Jean-Paul Belmondo is the Jean Valjean-like man who manages through good deeds to illuminate just how immoral and evil even the most sanctimonious people can be, and yet how some can be redeemed. This is a beautifully written film, directed with passion and color, and acted by all with transparent beauty. In French.

My Night at Maud's — (1969, directed by Eric Rohmer) Jean-Louis Trintignant is a footloose Catholic, if that's not an oxymoron, who confronts guilt and temptation during a possible one-night stand at Maud's house. You might call it a comedy for theologians. In French.

Persona — (1966, directed by Ingmar Bergman) A famous actress (Liv Ullmann) stops speaking in the middle of a performance and will not start again. The film deals with her summer of recuperation with a live-in nurse (Bibi Andersson), as they find odd identities in each others' personas. Bergman is at his best directing women, and these are two of his greatest actresses. In Swedish.

Ran — (1985, directed by Akira Kurosawa) This version of *King Lear* is set in medieval Japan, with a warlord's division of his fiefdom setting off escalating battles among his sons. There is beauty, and sadness, and extraordinary pageantry, and Kurosawa gives us battle scenes that were (badly) imitated by Mel Gibson in his 1995 film *Braveheart*. In Japanese.[4]

Run Lola Run — (1999, directed by Tom Tykwer) Not just the most delicious 80 minutes in film history, but a brilliant new way of making a movie. It's the story of how Lola tries to save her boyfriend from the clutches of the mob by coming up with 100,000 marks in twenty minutes. We see the whole thing three times, as Tykwer gives us three possible scenarios, including the life stories of people Lola meets on her way through town. If I were you I'd start with this one. In German.

Sansho the Bailiff — (1954, directed by Kenji Mizoguchi) In medieval Japan, as in Robin Hood's England, the bailiff (or sheriff) was a despot ruling over the local lands. Here he overpowers a provincial governor, takes his children as slaves, and sells his wife as a prostitute. The film tells their story — of agony and horror, and then of the restoration of justice. A masterpiece that's almost unknown in the United States. In Japanese.

[4] Someone asked Kurosawa how he managed to position his camera so as to show the sweep and range of his battle scenes. "Well," he said, "if I moved a bit to the right the Toshiba factory would be in the picture, and if I moved to the left we'd see the airport. So that's why I shot it where I did."

Scenes From a Marriage — (1973-74, directed by Ingmar Bergman) Exists in two forms: a six-hour television series, and a recut (by Bergman) 2½-hour theatrical version. Either of them is well worth your time, as Liv Ullmann and Erland Josephson (who cowrote it) play out the end of a marriage, the catharsis it brings, and the tentative reconnection that follows. Painful, moving, and ultimately even exhilarating. In Swedish.

The Seven Samurai — (1954, directed by Akira Kurosawa) A group of out-of-work samurai are hired by a village to protect it from marauding bandits. It's a classic western (later remade by John Sturges as *The Magnificent Seven*) that's slow to build but ultimately pays off in spades. Great fun, brilliant use of the camera by Kurosawa, and it has the charm of not taking cowardice too seriously. In Japanese.

The Seventh Seal — (1957, directed by Ingmar Bergman) A knight returns from ten years away at the Crusades, to find his country broken and desolated by the Black Plague. Death comes to take him, but he bargains for time by challenging him to a game of chess, during the playing of which he tries to find some hope, some sense that there is a meaning to life. Max von Sydow and Gunnar Bjornstrand are extraordinary as the knight and his squire. In Swedish.

Shoeshine — (1946, directed by Vittorio De Sica) Shot in Rome just after the war with non-actors, it's the story of two shoeshine boys trying to survive on the streets, who get involved in black marketeering, are arrested, and sent to a reformatory. Pauline Kael said, "If Mozart had written an opera set in poverty, it might have had this kind of painful beauty." A moving and powerful study of life on the edge. In Italian.

Stolen Kisses — (1968, directed by François Truffaut) The best of Truffaut's witty, semi-autobiographical films about a young jerk named Antoine Doinel stars Jean-Pierre Léaud as a lazy, charming guy who can't quite seem to get anything in his life to go the way it should. It vanishes from the mind pretty quickly, but you'll like it while you're watching it. In French.

The Trial of Joan of Arc — (1962, directed by Robert Bresson) Bresson began with the transcripts of the trial, and fleshed them out with scenes in her cell, and at her immolation, that are heartbreaking in their simple truths.

Cast mostly with amateurs, this deceptively simple film explores the great questions of conscience that underlie all our lives. In French.

Umberto D — (1952, directed by Vittorio De Sica) An almost unknown masterpiece about a retired civil servant trying to survive on a tiny pension, and knowing that he cannot. De Sica doesn't give us the easy out of making him lovable. Umberto is a difficult man, which makes his tragedy even more powerful. Cesare Zavattini's screenplay gives us enough in 90 minutes for a college course in society and the individual. In Italian.

I Vitelloni — (1953, directed by Federico Fellini) Pauline Kael translated the title as "Adolescent Slobs," and that's not a bad description of this autobiographical film. Four friends hang around, get into and out of trouble, learn about growing up. I like this because Fellini shows a casual wit and toughness that he lost in his later, overblown films. In Italian.

Weekend — (1967, directed by Jean-Luc Godard) This amazing film — part satire and part apocalypse — begins with a suburban couple leaving for a weekend visit to the wife's mother, and ends with the death of Western civilization. In between there's an erotic confession to a psychiatrist, a traffic jam that's one of the great sequences in the history of film, plus Alice in Wonderland, the French Revolution, urban guerrillas in the country, and a group of African garbage men who clean up the detritus. When it's over you won't believe what you just saw, but you'll love having seen it. In French.

Women on the Verge of a Nervous Breakdown — (1988, directed by Pedro Almodovar) An irresistible comedy about an actress whose longtime lover suddenly leaves her, and how she copes. The film moves like the wind, stopping only for some great gags and brilliant set-pieces. There's the taxi driver with a whole drug store in his cab, the bed-burning sequence, and best of all the gazpacho that saves the day. In Spanish.

Yojimbo — (1961, directed by Akira Kurosawa) Kurosawa had unwittingly created a monster with his portraits of the samurai as superhero, so he made this parody — of his own "Seven Samurai" and of the Toshiro Mifune character who exemplified it. Mifune is a down-at-the-heels samurai who comes upon a town that's divided into two warring camps. He plays one against the other until both are put in their place. Sergio Leone remade this as *A Fistful of Dollars*. In Japanese.

Z — (1969, directed by Costa-Gavras) This thriller is based on a true story, where an accidental death in Athens, and its investigation by an honest Greek bureaucrat, led to the uncovering of a Fascist conspiracy to take over the country — which actually happened. Extraordinary performances by Yves Montand and Jean-Louis Trintignant. Shot in Algeria, in French.

MYSTERIES

People sometimes mistake a suspense film for a mystery — a mystery is something that's unraveled in the course of the movie, while a suspense film depends on the audience's tension while fearing the unknown — but there are wonderful films in both genres. Alfred Hitchcock said that suspense is better than mystery, and for him that was true, but there are some marvelous mystery films that you can enjoy just as much. Here are the essential ones, of both types.

The Maltese Falcon — (1941, directed by John Huston) A comic mystery, one of the most perfect films ever made. Humphrey Bogart is Sam Spade, trying to solve the mystery of his partner's death; this film defined his screen persona for all time. You'll meet Sydney Greenstreet and Peter Lorre in their first pairing, as shady characters in search of the elusive falcon. Huston wrote the script from the Dashiell Hammett novel, and there's wonderful film-noir lighting by cameraman Arthur Edeson. This is one of those miracles you can see a hundred times and still love every minute.

The Big Sleep — (1946, directed by Howard Hawks) Bogart again, this time as Raymond Chandler's detective Philip Marlowe, trying to help Lauren Bacall and her out-of-control sister deal with a blackmailer. Nobel laureate William Faulkner worked on the script and there's still one murder no one is too sure about, but things move so fast you'll never notice.[5] Pure back-lot production, and all the better for it.

The Lady Vanishes — (1938, directed by Alfred Hitchcock) One of the most delicious mystery/suspense/comedies ever, this witty film begins with the disappearance of a lovely old lady (Dame May Whitty) from a train in central Europe, on the eve of World War II. Two passengers join forces to find her, get involved with international intrigue, and even find romance.

---

[5] Faulkner was a screenwriter for many Hollywood films, and Hawks once invited him and Clark Gable for a fishing trip in the Sierra Nevadas. Gable, no intellectual, said, "What do you do, Mr. Faulkner?" A pause. "I'm a writer, Mr. Gable. What do you do?"

Many funny moments and some nicely scary ones add to the pleasure of the film. Unlike most other Hitchcocks, this one has a whole gallery of interesting characters.

The 39 Steps — (1935, directed by Alfred Hitchcock) Another witty classic, with innocent Robert Donat finding himself in the middle of a spy-and murder mystery, pursued up and down the length of the British Isles by both the spy ring and the police, half the time handcuffed to delightful Madeleine Carroll (don't ask). From the John Buchan novel. There are at least a half-dozen classic Hitchcock moments for you to savor.

Double Indemnity — (1944, directed by Billy Wilder) Raymond Chandler collaborated with Wilder to write a perfect script from the James M. Cain novel, and the suspense is unbearable. Barbara Stanwyck gets husband Fred MacMurray involved in a murder-for-insurance-money scheme, and investigator Edward G. Robinson is assigned to the case. Maybe the most completely satisfying suspense film ever made. Extraordinary performances by Stanwyck and Robinson.

The Thin Man — (1934, directed by W.S. Van Dyke) Oh, for the days when stars could drink and drink and joke and joke and still solve murder mysteries. Meet Nick and Nora Charles (and their dog Asta), who do all of those things, many of them at the same time. William Powell and Myrna Loy are the perfect couple in this first of the series, from the Dashiell Hammett novel.

After the Thin Man — (1936, directed by W.S. Van Dyke) Second in the series, this is even richer in plot, and actually gives us young James Stewart as a suspect. Martinis are still poured at every possible occasion, and a good time is had by all.

The Silence of the Lambs — (1991, directed by Jonathan Demme) Almost unbearably powerful and scary story of FBI trainee Jodie Foster who must work with brilliant imprisoned murderer Hannibal "The Cannibal" Lecter — Anthony Hopkins — to get insights into the mind and location of a frightful serial killer, and their bargain leads to the best and wittiest last line in years. Everybody won Oscars, deservedly.

L.A. Confidential — (1997, directed by Curtis Hanson) A remarkable mystery, rich with overtones of corruption, bigotry, pornography, and media sleaze, that follows a group of Los Angeles detectives in the 1950s as they work on an ever-increasing series of murders around town. Hanson holds this sprawling story together by taking his time and giving his actors room to breathe. Maybe the climax is too apocalyptic, but you won't care.

ONE-OF-A-KINDS

These are films that seem to stand outside all genres. You could say they emerged from the minds of their creators whole and without antecedents, somehow got produced — in some cases because the filmmakers owned the studio or had the money to make them independently — and have survived long enough to command our attention. They're included here not necessarily because of overall intrinsic value, but because it's important for the movies, like any art form, to honor their eccentrics.

Brazil — (1985, directed by Terry Gilliam) A variation on "1984," with overtones of Kafka, where a conventional bureaucrat's life is overturned by powers that he cannot reach or even communicate with. Jonathan Pryce is the protagonist, Robert DeNiro is a kind of Mr. Fixit, and Pryce's dreams of escape (to Brazil) are more and more powerful. Some superb moments, great sets and art direction, but the story just got away from Gilliam.

Chelsea Girls — (1966, directed by Andy Warhol) A remarkable documentary of Warhol's friends at play and otherwise in a series of scenes, shot at New York's Chelsea Hotel in 16mm and designed to be projected (by two projectors) onto two screens simultaneously, so that you can choose to watch either scene or both at once. This is the last film he directed himself, and it is his best.

Fantasia — (1940, many credits) Begin with a man who knows little about music (Walt Disney), add the overblown Leopold Stokowski as his music guru, fill in with two hours of full animation (later cut to 90 minutes) as only the Disney studio could do it, and you end up with, thank God, the one, the only, *Fantasia*. Not for the faint of heart or delicate of stomach, but you have to see it once to know how wrong a film can go. You'll hate yourself for enjoying it, but you will enjoy it.

It's a Wonderful Life — (1946, directed by Frank Capra) Listed here because there's no category for romances, which is what this is. It's crammed full of everything you ever wanted in a movie: good people, bad people, strength, weakness, love, forgiveness, and best of all the knowledge that if you killed yourself the world would be a much worse place. What more could you want? You'll laugh, you'll cry, you'll cry, you'll cry. See it every Christmas.

Lola Montes — (1955, directed by Max Ophuls) Max Ophuls could make a camera do things no one else dared to try, and this story of a circus artist (Martine Carol) and her lovers gave him the space to make sweeping, swooping, circling shots like you've never seen before. But Carol, who should ooze sex appeal as Lola, is flat and boring in the lead, and even Peter Ustinov's sophisticated narration can't carry the film. Still, worth seeing for the chance to watch a forgotten master at work. In English and French.

The Man with the Movie Camera — (1929, directed by Dziga Vertov) Almost unknown for many years except to film students and scholars, this was made in the giddiest days of Soviet film experimentation, yet there's no political content at all. It's a tour de force, an encyclopedia, of movie techniques, many invented by Vertov and his cameraman Mikhail Kaufman for this film, that were never seen again until the New Wave thirty years later. It's a film about a camera telling us what it sees, in and around a city, on an ordinary day, and showing us what extraordinary things a motion picture camera can do.

One From the Heart — (1982, directed by Francis Ford Coppola) One of the strangest films ever made, and certainly unlike anything else by Coppola, this is a surreal fantasy of a trip to Las Vegas, but a Vegas composed and created on a back lot with music. Half the time you won't believe what you're seeing, the other half you'll be enchanted. The legendary Dean Tavoularis created the sets, and the also legendary Vittorio Storaro shot it.

Robin and Marian — (1976, directed by Richard Lester) Did you ever think about what happened to the famous pair after good King Richard was restored to power and Robin and Marian had grown old? Sean Connery and Audrey Hepburn play the aging couple with wit and fire and a marvelous melancholy. A wonderfully bold attempt to put a realistic spin on the legend, that doesn't demean either the legend or the characters.

Sunset Boulevard — (1950, directed by Billy Wilder) This bleak yet utterly compelling black comedy/drama gives us the formerly beauteous Norma Desmond (Gloria Swanson) as what Swanson was in reality — an aging silent-film star fantasizing her way to a comeback film. Erich von Stroheim is her butler, though he once was her husband and her director; and William Holden is the pathetic screenwriter who tells us the story. "I'm ready for my closeup, Mr. DeMille."

EPICS

Epics have been around since D.W. Griffith made *The Birth of a Nation* in 1915, but I'm still not quite sure what makes an epic and what just makes a gaseous bloat. The epic is a nineteenth-century construct, and it sits uneasily in a twentieth-century art form. The medium looks forward, while the sensibility looks back. There's a terrible temptation to substitute tableau for motion, and cliché for insight. And since epics deal with stories everybody knows already, there's a dreadful sense of déja vu that's hard to overcome. When Pauline Kael was describing Abel Gance's 1927 epic *Napoleon*, which begins with a section on Napoleon's childhood, she pointed out that if Part 2 showed us the Man of Destiny, Part 1 — with Napoleon leading his outnumbered schoolmates in a snowball fight — gave us the Boy of Destiny. It seems as though the epic can work only if the people in it are grounded in reality and their conflicts are on a human scale. Here are the ones that fit.

Gone With the Wind — (1939, directed by Victor Fleming) The classic epic, it triumphs because it's actually built around the relationships, conflicts, and passions the main characters have for each other. Reduce them to stereotypes or clichés and the heart would be cut out of the film. The dialogue is pithy and fresh, the acting is brilliant, certainly by Vivien Leigh and Clark Gable, and enough happens to carry this soap opera over the top and into the realm of the sublime.

Spartacus — (1960, directed by Stanley Kubrick) Probably the last of the left-wing, socially-conscious films to make an impact on Americans, it follows Kirk Douglas as the gladiator-slave who leads a revolt against the decadent, proto-fascist Roman state. Some breathtaking battlefield scenes, balanced by both eloquent talk of the rights of man and by wonderfully perverse scenes of evil people enjoying themselves.

Lawrence of Arabia — (1962, directed by David Lean) Essence of epic. Great sweeping vistas across the desert, a flawed British hero who lives for adventure (Peter O'Toole) and a traditional Arab hero as his foil (Omar Sharif), this is a film peopled with marvelous characters who all follow their own needs and drives. It never makes quite clear just why the good guys are better than the bad guys, but nobody really cares.

Titanic — (1997, directed by James Cameron) The most expensive — and most profitable — film ever made, it is a pure adolescent fantasy of love and death on the very largest possible scale. Awesome though overly repetitious special effects convey both the beauty of being on board the great ship and the horror one feels at facing death by drowning, and an exciting performance by Leonardo DiCaprio as the wild colonial boy who pursues the girl of his dreams make it worthwhile, as does the imaginative contemporary bookend that Cameron gives us through the eyes of an aged survivor.

SHAKESPEARE ON FILM

When it comes to producing Shakespeare on film, many are called, usually by their egos, but few are chosen. Plays that can be magical on stage, that have spoken so truly to every part of our lives for almost four hundred years that they still have the power to astonish and delight and frighten and move us beyond measure, keep finding themselves hacked to pieces, misread by egomaniacs, and presented to us as some kind of "new revelation." Of course it's not easy to do Shakespeare right. What's needed for any production is an entire cast of exquisitely good actors who can read Shakespeare as he was meant to be read, but who also understand that communicating on film is not the same as communicating on stage (see Chapter 2). Then you must have a director who knows where and when to open the action up — to a ship, a battlefield, a castle rampart — without stepping all over what Shakespeare already created. And last, the director must have the wit to recognize that Shakespeare was a better writer than he or she is, and that the lines themselves are the ultimate joy of the plays; when the words and speeches work, the characters will take care of themselves. It's a tough job, and most people screw it up. Here is my selection of those who got it at least mostly right, plus one who got it half-right.

Richard III — (1955, directed by Laurence Olivier) Of his three Shakespeare films (the others are *Hamlet* and *Henry V*) this one has the delicious pleasure of watching the greatest villain in theatre history stalk the castle in pursuit of the crown. Olivier was never better, wooing Claire Bloom just moments after having her husband killed, destroying the hopes of retainers ("I am not in the giving mood today"), while still — the key to this play — making Richard irresistibly attractive to us in the audience.

Macbeth — (1948, directed by Orson Welles) Executives at Republic Pictures, home of the second-rate western, never knew what hit them when Welles shot this brilliant version of Shakespeare's most melodramatic play, on a couple of their sound stages. With nothing but whatever was around in the form of platforms, steps, shapes, props, and killer lighting, he created everything from a king's bedroom to a banquet hall to a battlefield. Chopped to pieces and later dubbed in part, much of Welles's power — and that exquisitely compelling voice — still survives.

Twelfth Night — (1996, directed by Trevor Nunn) This seemingly simple play, done by every high school drama department for its farcical elements, is actually a dark and thoughtful examination of who we are and who we wish we were. Nunn's version has all the wit and gags, but also finds the beauty and sadness of failed and unfulfilled lives. Imogen Stubbs, Helena Bonham Carter, and Ben Kingsley (as Feste) do honor to this production.

Hamlet — (1996, directed by Kenneth Branagh) Branagh was brave enough to give us this uncut four-hour version, and talented enough to carry it off in the title role. The film is well paced, and there is time for us to learn all that Shakespeare has to tell us about life and death at Elsinore, but Branagh has made two bad decisions: One is an inexplicable rush to a jumbled finale, and the other is the woeful miscasting of a group of American "guest stars" in minor roles. Still, it's important to see it performed as Shakespeare wrote it.

Romeo & Juliet — (1996, directed by Baz Luhrmann) This is a production of the quintessential teenage love story as conceived and directed for the screen by a 35-year-old teenager. Half of it is breathtaking, with incredibly kinetic scenes of love and rage in a contemporary city run by two competing families, and a heartbreaking performance by Claire Danes as Juliet. The other half is a sappy performance by the puerile Leonardo DiCaprio, who fails to capture any of what makes Romeo worth loving. But the final sequence in the church will take your breath away. It's one of the great shots of all time.

WAR FILMS

I grew up on John Wayne-type war films: doomed or triumphant heroes holding off the hated Japanese or German hordes with one last hand grenade or torpedo or burst of machine-gun fire. If I were to include any of them (*Bataan*, *Back to Bataan*, *Wake Island*, and the like) I'd have to put them in a special Fantasy category. Rather than do that, let's just skip to the war films that have some resonance for those of us who live in the real world.

The Battle of Algiers — (1965, directed by Gillo Pontecorvo) This is an astonishing film — a kind of recreated documentary — about the Algerian revolt against France from 1954 to 1962. Shot (in Tunisia) in a kind of newsreel, hidden-camera style, it builds along with the revolt, guerrilla cell by guerrilla cell, until there is all-out war. At the same time, it gives us a fascinating and not unsympathetic profile of the French counterinsurrection chief whose job is to stop the revolution at any cost.

Platoon — (1986, directed by Oliver Stone) It seems to take a bad war to make a good film. Life on the line in Vietnam was nasty, brutish, and short, and this film shows us why. Stone based the script on his own experience there, directed with a sure and not-overwrought hand, and got fine performances from a believable cast.

Paths of Glory — (1957, directed by Stanley Kubrick) This is the story of an obscene episode in World War I, where a French general tried to cover up his own disastrous ineptitude by blaming those under him. Kirk Douglas plays a courageous officer who tries to prevent the tragedy. The moral questions are well handled without obstructing the story.

Schindler's List — (1993, directed by Steven Spielberg) The immensity of the Holocaust still defeats us, but it can be confronted when broken down into more manageable pieces. Spielberg takes Thomas Keneally's novel of an unlikely hero — a Nazi war profiteer who ran a slave-labor factory and yet managed to save thousands of Jews from the gas chambers — and brings his audience through the apocalypse and out the other side into redemption.

Dr. Strangelove — (1964, directed by Stanley Kubrick) I put this film here instead of with the comedies for two reasons: a) it's about soldiers, even if they are generals; and b) it's not funny. Kubrick could no more direct a comedy than Bergman could, but this survives his lack of wit because the script is so outrageous. Maybe Quentin Tarantino will do the remake.

Saving Private Ryan — (1998, directed by Steven Spielberg) The most extraordinary combat footage ever shot outside of combat both opens and closes this film about the first few days of the Normandy landings in 1944, and for this alone the film must be seen. Tom Hanks as the English teacher turned platoon leader gives his thoughtful performance as an everyman, but the film is underwritten when it comes to letting us know the participants, and settles for a cheap dramatic device to deal with the coward in the group.

DOCUMENTARIES

Documentaries have never found an audience in the United States. I think of two reasons: First, television has been able to offer live, often uninflected coverage of everything from war to murder trials, particularly these days on cable networks devoted to those subjects; and second, because television news, with its prepackaged, predigested stories — news, sports, weather — delivered every hour of every day — undercuts the market for longer, more thoughtful examinations of our lives and our world. And when documentarians have been admitted to the celebrity of public honor, it's been for their work in areas that are no longer controversial, like the Ken Burns documentaries on baseball, the Civil War, the Lewis & Clark expedition, and the like.

Nevertheless, filmmakers and video makers continue to work, continue to offer us their eyes and ears and understanding of life and society and the world, in hopes that we will take something away with us, and perhaps even learn something as well. Here are my own selections.

Best Boy — (1979, directed by Ira Wohl) This is a loving and poignant study of Wohl's mentally retarded adult cousin Philly, who lives with his aging parents. The question they face of making plans for Philly's life after they have died is set against the daily activities and special events they share, including a wonderful visit backstage with Zero Mostel, where he and Zero sing a duet of "If I Were a Rich Man." In 1997 Wohl made a followup film, revisiting Philly as he found him twenty years later.

Don't Look Back — (1967, directed by D.A. Pennebaker) A look at the charming and not-so-charming young Bob Dylan, on tour through the British Isles in 1965 with Joan Baez in tow as his groupie, this is the perfect example of cinema-verité filmmaking. Some wonderful performances of the early songs, plus the famous sequence of Dylan holding the lyric cards while doing "Subterranean Homesick Blues." That's Allen Ginsberg in the background.

Harlan County USA — (1977, directed by Barbara Kopple) If Kopple had been around to record the bloody mining strikes of the thirties, the course of American history might have been changed. Here she shows us a latter-day example of corporate union-busting, a mentality that learned nothing in the intervening forty years. She follows the strikers and their families (they sing "Union Maid" and "Which Side Are You On"), during the course of a long and bloody strike in this quintessential home of goons, ginks, and company finks.

Hearts of Darkness — (1991, directed by Fax Bahr and George Hickenlooper) Utilizing footage shot by Francis Ford Coppola's wife/ex-wife during the disastrous filming of *Apocalypse Now*, combined with subsequent interviews with many of the participants, this gives us an idea of the kind of catastrophe that only the greatest filmmakers can bring on themselves. Absolutely the very best film ever made about filmmaking.

Pumping Iron — (1977, directed by George Butler and Robert Fiore) A witty and fascinating study of the 1975 Mr. Olympia world bodybuilding competition, which came down to a contest of wills and talent between Arnold Schwarzenegger and Lou Ferrigno. Watch how the brilliant Schwarzenegger psyches out his rival by using his knowledge of personalities and their weaknesses, matched by a remarkable understanding of himself and his own abilities.

Roger and Me — (1989, directed by Michael Moore) A sardonic look at 1980s capitalism in America, as it follows Moore's odyssey trying to locate and meet with Roger Smith, the CEO of General Motors, who has just closed down the Chevrolet factory in Flint, Michigan and thrown the whole city into disaster. An insight into the bloodshed behind the bloodless word "downsized."

The Sorrow and the Pity — (1970, directed by Marcel Ophuls) This is little more than four and a half hours of interviews with French men and women who were on both sides during World War II, and yet it is everything. The revelations by collaborators about what they did, including their insistent and continuing anti-Semitism, lead one to suspect that France and Germany are like two sides of the same coin. At the same time, the recollections of those who worked in the Resistance are almost enough to right the balance. An eloquent document of testimony by those who were there.

Streetwise — (1984, directed by Martin Bell) Meet the homeless children of Seattle, in Martin Bell's frank and heart-rending film. They live on the streets, have "dates" with whomever will at least agree to feed them a meal and let them sleep in a bed, they sicken and even die as we watch. It's hard to imagine a more powerful indictment of the values and priorities of contemporary America. Leonard Maltin suggests that this would make "a telling double bill with any one of a dozen idiotic adolescent comedies" of the era. Better yet, it should be required viewing by all members of Congress.

The Times of Harvey Milk — (1984, directed by Robert Epstein) This is a portrait of Milk, the gay activist from the Sunset district who ran for and was elected as a City of San Francisco Supervisor, and then was murdered by a fellow Supervisor because he was gay. A beautiful film that tells the story without rancor, it lets us enjoy getting to know Milk in life, so that we can mourn his death more deeply.

Titicut Follies — (1967, directed by Frederick Wiseman) Wiseman, a lawyer turned documentary filmmaker, was allowed access to this Massachusetts institution for the criminally insane. "The Titicut Follies" are the annual revue put on by inmates and staff. Not an exposé of a snake pit, it shows us problems that are even deeper, and more reflective of how yesterday's wisdom can't solve today's issues.

Welfare — (1975, directed by Frederick Wiseman) Wiseman simply turned his camera onto life at a Manhattan welfare office, and observed the interactions between staff and clients. This is a real-life cross between *1984* and *Catch-22*, with the office personnel opening and closing their service windows and counters at will, managing to misdirect their clients all over town without helping them, and finding unnumbered ways — not all deliberate by any means — to humiliate and anger them.

ADVENTURES

The movies were made for adventure. Westerns, cartoons, period pieces and fantasies all are adventures of one sort or another, and they've deservedly drawn the largest audiences over the years. But there's also a category of films that are truly adventures; that is, they're about an adventure that their protagonists experience; and they are exciting and satisfying for the very tingle of daring and danger we feel as we watch them.

Adventures of Robin Hood — (1938, directed by Michael Curtiz and William Keighley; Curtiz replaced Keighley in mid-shoot) This is the classic swashbuckler, Errol Flynn's greatest role, in fact the role that defined all his later performances. Watch and thrill as he swashbuckles his way through Sherwood Forest, slinging a deer over his shoulder (try it sometime), loving Olivia de Havilland, duelling evil Basil Rathbone, matching wits with that no-good Claude Rains.

The Man Who Would Be King — (1975, directed by John Huston) Huston had this script for twenty years, but no one would finance it. Extraordinary casting of the short story by Kipling, set at the turn of the twentieth century: Sean Connery and Michael Caine play two British adventurers who try to steal the riches of the Himalayan country of Kafiristan, by palming off Connery as its rightful king. Wild and beautiful, sometimes very witty, and ultimately poignant.

Raiders of the Lost Ark — (1981, directed by Steven Spielberg) The first and best of the Indiana Jones series, with Harrison Ford moving on from his Han Solo persona to take over a film by himself. The lost ark is, of course, the ark of the covenant, which Moses himself, etc., etc., so you can see why it's important that Indy find it. Along the way he meets and conquers more traps, assassins, and generally bad types than have ever been assembled in one 2-hour movie in history. Great fun.

The Thief of Bagdad — (1940, six directors worked on it; three are credited) Sabu is the boy thief who comes to the aid of the prince who's been blinded by the evil usurper Conrad Veidt; with the help of the old silent movie actor Rex Ingram as a wonderful genie, and with flying carpet rides and a whole panoply of great special effects, justice finally is done. Fabulous sets and costumes, fully worthy of the Arabian Nights.

The Wizard of Oz — (1939, directed by Victor Fleming, though King Vidor also directed but was uncredited) More than an adventure, more than a musical, this is one of those miracles that the movies produce from time to time. The great songs by Harold Arlen and Yip Harburg reveal inner thoughts and feelings as well as move the plot along. There's not a weak link anywhere — not in acting, singing, script, sets, or costumes. This is as close to perfection as a film can come, and probably should be seen once a year just as a special treat.

SCIENCE FICTION

The very early film pioneer Georges Méliès, who by the year 1900 had invented the dissolve, the double exposure and the fade, also invented the science fiction film. His *Voyage to the Moon*, featuring a rocket launch and a direct hit on the nose of the Man in the Moon, is still available for viewing. Since then there have been many technical advances, but the truly fine films — where the story is worth doing, where the implications for humans are explored, or where the sheer excitement of the film takes over — are much rarer than we would like. Here are the essential ones.

E.T. the Extraterrestrial — (1982, directed by Steven Spielberg) Poignant and funny, this Spielberg classic will live as a fable with the message that, as one 5-year-old I know put it, "Grownups don't always know what's right." No kidding. Beautifully put together by Spielberg to give us a family in disarray confronting a benign and very cute extraterrestrial who is NOT omnipotent or omniscient, who in fact will die if he cannot get back to his own world. The enemy here is our own government, and the power of the film lies in the ability of the children to outwit it.

Frankenstein — (1931, directed by James Whale) The one, the original, the 1931 film that made Boris Karloff's monster a household image, and lurching a boy's rite of passage. In 1987 some originally censored scenes were restored, importantly the sequence in which a little girl is drowned, and the film gains power from them.

The Invasion of the Body Snatchers — (1956, directed by Don Siegel) Still a provocative examination of a society where almost everyone is too bland to exert any moral force, or care about good and evil, in effect becoming vegetable pod people, who look and sound just like us, but who will destroy everything worthwhile in our society. At the time, nobody got that this was an allegory of McCarthyism and a refusal to think for oneself. But you will.

The Invisible Man — (1933, directed by James Whale) The H.G. Wells story of the scientist who discovers a potion that will make him invisible; it also makes him into a mad murderer. Simple but wonderful, and watching Claude Rains wrap and unwrap himself with bandages so as to be either seen or unseen is a scary delight.

The Sixth Sense — (1999, directed by M. Night Shyamalan) A sleeper that almost wasn't released by the studio but went on to make hundreds of millions of dollars. Shyamalan tells the perfect ghost story, using a beautifully understated performance by Bruce Willis, and a heartbreaking one by the 9-year-old Haley Joel Osment. With Toni Collette as Osment's mother.

The Star Wars Trilogy — (*Star Wars:* 1977, directed by George Lucas; *The Empire Strikes Back:* 1980, directed by Irvin Kershner; *The Return of the Jedi:* 1983, directed by Richard Marquand) One of the amazing things about these three films, by three different directors, is how alike they are stylistically. Lucas kept a very firm hand on all of them as producer (and uncredited co-director of the last two). A wonderfully pulpy story that might have come right out of the pages of *Amazing Stories* magazine, it makes three brilliantly realized films, perfectly cast, richly produced, with enormous care given to everything from Darth Vader to Yoda to the Ewoks.

NEXT WAVE

For some reason, the idea of calling something new in movies a wave hasn't yet been devalued by overuse. In fact, as far as I know there have been only two "waves" in all of movie history. The first swept over us around 1960, the New Wave, when we were confronted with an amazing group of films from a group of young French filmmakers, films that destroyed our conventional notions of what a narrative movie should be and changed the way all films have been made ever since. The second, which for want of a better term I'll call the Next Wave, came in 1994, with Quentin Tarantino's *Pulp Fiction*. In just a few years it has spawned a whole group of stylistically related films that share a number of attributes — chief among them being a population of picaresque characters, viewed from an ironic directorial distance, combined with a welcome amorality that won't separate "good guys" from "bad guys", and coupled at their best with very nice dry wit. Here are the ones you need to see. Note that *L.A. Confidential* is a member of this group, but by virtue of being a mystery it is listed in that category instead.

Pulp Fiction — (1994, directed by Quentin Tarantino) The classic next wave film, it is close to perfection as it follows two killers, two thieves, a boxer, their boss, and the boss's wife through a day and a night, or is that a night and a day, like none you've ever seen before. Chronologically Tarantino manages to end the film in the middle, which is where it belongs. And you'll never forget the Royale, the breast-plate injection, Honeybunny, or Jack Rabbit Slim's. The most exciting influence on films since Godard's *Weekend*.

Jackie Brown — (1997, directed by Quentin Tarantino) An aging flight attendant without much to look forward to (the old blaxploitation star Pam Grier) is a "mule" for an L.A. crook, carrying for him on her run to and from Cabo San Lucas. The movie is filled with wonderfully observed people involved in a series of crosses, double crosses, triple crosses, and God knows what else. The pleasure of the film is that every character is enjoyable to watch, no matter who's doing what to whom. Perfectly paced and spacious enough to spend time on even the smallest details, it's convincing evidence that *Pulp Fiction* wasn't a one-shot fluke. Film buffs will love the breathtaking crane shot, an homage to Orson Welles. Everyone will love the performances by Samuel L. Jackson and Robert DeNiro.

The Usual Suspects — (1995, directed by Bryan Singer) A Chinese-box puzzle built on the lineup of five suspects hauled in to a New York police station for questioning, which turns into a fascinating sequence of strange and murderous conspiracies in Los Angeles that leave us always a step or two behind the events. It was Kevin Spacey's breakthrough film — he won an Oscar as the whiny suspect with a clubfoot.

DRAMAS

Some of these are among the finest films of the century, regardless of genre. They're quintessentially American (yes, even *Amadeus*), and like the best fiction they have enough power and beauty and drive to keep you thinking about them at even the most unexpected times. You'll find yourself comparing every movie you see from now on to one or another of them.

All About Eve — (1950, directed by Joseph L. Mankiewicz) Mankiewicz also wrote the script for this elegant story of theatrical infighting, about an aging star, played with power and wit by Bette Davis, who's confronted with a rapacious young woman who may take her place. The dialogue is overloaded with rapier attacks and parries, and epigrams are tossed back and forth like ping-pong balls.

Amadeus — (1984, directed by Milos Forman) The story of Mozart's life in Vienna, as told by his rival, the elegant and mediocre court composer Salieri. The sublime music becomes a counterpoint to the drama and gathering tragedy, but there is wit and beauty throughout. Brilliant acting by F. Murray Abraham as Salieri and Tom Hulce as the wonderfully boorish Mozart. Notice the staging of scenes from the operas, done by the great Twyla Tharp.

Barton Fink — (1991, directed by Joel Coen) An unappreciated masterpiece. The Coens take a Clifford Odets-type New York-intellectual-left-wing playwright (John Turturro) to Hollywood in 1940, where the studio puts him up in a hotel, and then puts him to work writing scripts for Wallace Beery instead of saving humanity. Along the way he meets John Goodman, his hotel neighbor, who in a breathtaking performance takes Turturro — and us — right into the apocalypse.

Casablanca — (1942, directed by Michael Curtiz) The story of a cynic redeemed by love, this may be the most enjoyable film ever made. Bogart and Bergman are so sexy together they don't even have to get undressed. Great lines galore come one after another "I came to Casablanca for the waters." "Waters? What waters? We're in the middle of the desert." "I was misinformed," and let's all say the last line together: "Louie, this is the start of a beautiful friendship."

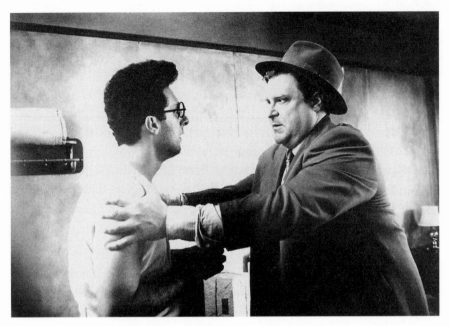

John Turturro listens to John Goodman's story in *Barton Fink*.

Citizen Kane — (1941, directed by Orson Welles) Everything was different about this film, starting with its structure: a reporter asks a simple question about the dead media tycoon's last word ("Rosebud"), and we're off on a search for understanding the life of Charles Foster Kane from childhood to the grave. We move backward and forward in time, putting pieces together. Welles of course is Kane, in a breathtaking performance that dominates the film as his character did in life. The shots, the lighting, and the editing have been studied in every film school as examples of inventive yet appropriate techniques.

Dead Man Walking — (1995, directed by Tim Robbins) From the book by Sister Helen Préjean, Susan Sarandon becomes the spiritual advisor to Sean Penn, convicted of a double murder and rape and sitting on death row in Louisiana. The film takes its time, letting us get to know Penn's character as well as Helen's, along with the parents of the murdered couple. The death penalty is the ultimate paradox, and the film burns through us by asking what is justice and what is right. Sarandon won an Oscar, but Penn gives one of the great film performances of all time.

Field of Dreams — (1989, directed by Phil Alden Robinson) The eighties' answer to *It's a Wonderful Life*, from the book *Shoeless Joe* by W.P. Kinsella. You'll cry with joy at the climax of this marvelously sentimental story of a failure who in trying to connect with the dead baseball hero finds his way to reconnect with his own father. It's about the power of magic, and the magic really works. Kevin Costner is gloriously right in the role.

From Here to Eternity — (1953, directed by Fred Zinneman) Army life around Pearl Harbor just before the Japanese attack. Yes, there's the famous shot of Burt Lancaster and Deborah Kerr rolling around in the surf, but the breathtaking surprise for those who never saw him in his prime is the brilliant acting of Frank Sinatra as Maggio, the man who won't take shit. The film is so believable, so haunting, that certain episodes will stay with you all your life.

The Godfather — (1972, directed by Francis Ford Coppola) Without doubt the most perfect film ever made. A script that allows its plot to grow out of its characters, acting that reveals all yet rewards repeated viewing, and direction that enabled every actor to go far beyond anything they had done before. And then the brilliant photography and lighting by Gordon Willis, and the haunting music by Nino Rota, add mood and power to the film. You must own this one.

The Godfather, Part II — (1974, directed by Francis Ford Coppola) Coppola and Puzo give us more of the Corleones, going back to immigrant days and forward to Havana in the late 50s, with Robert DeNiro appearing as the young Don, and then following Michael (Pacino) after he's taken over the family. Maybe only the third or fourth greatest film of all time, but still worth your attention.

Great Expectations — (1946, directed by David Lean) A poor orphan grows up with the assistance of — well, who? — and deals with life and love along the way. The meeting in the graveyard between young Pip and the ex-con Finlay Currie is one of the great moments in film. Strengthened by the extraordinary talent of every actor, a classic British group, this is a pleasure to watch from beginning to end.

Sean Penn and Susan Sarandon in *Dead Man Walking*.

The Magnificent Ambersons — (1942, directed by Orson Welles) Welles's second film and a complete reversal of course from *Citizen Kane*. Taken from the Booth Tarkington novel about an Indiana family living through the changes at the turn of the twentieth century, and how they deal with them. More brilliant shot-making, and a deeper understanding of what makes people tick. Welles left for South America and the studio had the hack Robert Wise reshoot and recut the ending. They couldn't get rid of the genius, though.

Malcolm X — (1992, directed by Spike Lee) Denzel Washington gives the performance of a lifetime as Malcolm, a man of genius and eloquence, taking us on his journey from pimp and dealer through his years in prison to his apotheosis as the voice of black (and white) conscience in America. An amazing film, marred only by a shallow and distorted presentation, in its middle section, of Malcolm's conversion and resurrection.

Rocky — (1976, directed by John Avildsen) Don't laugh. It's not Stallone's fault that everybody's latched onto the concept and the music. This film is close to perfect, the story of a not-very-bright club fighter who gets the chance to fight the champion. Stallone wrote the script and created a believable character, and director Avildsen was right to let all the emotion hang out.

Who's Afraid of Virginia Woolf? — (1966, directed by Mike Nichols) If you ever wondered whether Elizabeth Taylor was more than just a pair of gorgeous violet eyes, be sure to see this. She was truly an actress, and shows it here in this overlong but still powerful version of Albee's play. A great performance in an unbearably difficult role as a harridan castrator of her husband (Richard Burton in an unfamiliar role).

WESTERNS

Did you ever stop to think how weird it is that there's a whole genre of westerns? Perhaps the west does for us what Troy did for Greece. Western heroes are our demigods, as Achilles and Hector were for the Greeks. There are hardly any westerns that don't have heroes and a heroic component, white or Indian, and with good reason. How can you have mythology without the gods?

A Fistful of Dollars — (1964, directed by Sergio Leone) This remake of Kurosawa's *Yojimbo* turns the story into opera, with Leone showing what became his trademark gestures, like Cinemascope closeups of a pair of eyes, or Clint Eastwood "The Man With No Name" lighting one of his little cigars. A truly romantic version of the western myth, even though it was shot in Spain, and lots of fun besides. The first "spaghetti Western."

Once Upon a Time in the West — (1968, directed by Sergio Leone) A wonderful climax to Leone's western series, he actually turns the genre's conventions on their head by casting Henry Fonda(!) as the arch-villain. Gorgeous, leisurely, a pleasure to watch; and Ennio Morricone's music adds enormously to its power. Trivia note: Bernardo Bertolucci worked on the script with Leone.

Stagecoach — (1939, directed by John Ford) There's a possibly apocryphal story that Orson Welles was asked how he learned about filmmaking. He said: "From the old masters — John Ford, John Ford, and John Ford." This is the film that made John Wayne a star, giving him a backstory (he's a convict on his way to jail) and even a love interest, sort of (Claire Trevor). Beautifully shot in Monument Valley, and edited without a wasted moment.

SPORTS FILMS

What you do not need is any of those inspirational bioflicks about Lou Gehrig, the Babe, or other figures from the mythological past. What you do need is movies that are really and truly sports flicks, whether they're fantasy or not.

Bull Durham — (1988, directed by Ron Shelton) Except for the fact that Tim Robbins is badly miscast as a fireball pitcher, since his fastball comes up to the plate about the same speed as my great-aunt Elsa's, this is a wonderful movie about life in and around the minor leagues. Kevin Costner is perfect as the sophisticated catcher who can't make it up to the major leagues, and Susan Sarandon is the team groupie. Great moments, particularly the conferences on the mound.

A League of their Own — (1992, directed by Penny Marshall) Underrated at the time, this is a witty and thoughtful piece of filmmaking about the women's baseball league that started during World War II. Beautifully acted by a talented ensemble, particularly Geena Davis as the team's star, Madonna as the team sexpot, and Jon Lovitz as a scout. The cast can actually play, and play hard and well; and the framing device to cover the actual induction of the real women of the league, now in their sixties and seventies, into the Hall of Fame at Cooperstown, will bring tears to your eyes.

Personal Best — (1982, directed by Robert Towne) Overrated at the time because of its then-daring lesbian theme, this film has settled down as a good study of how life and love and sex impinge on an athlete's preparation for world-class competition. Mariel Hemingway is the track star training for the 1980 Olympics, Scott Glenn makes the most of a stereotypical role as the sexist, controlling coach.

White Men Can't Jump — (1992, directed by Ron Shelton) Pure fun in the sun, with Wesley Snipes and Woody Harrelson as playground basketball hustlers, making money in halfcourt 2-on-2 games with the unsuspecting locals; and delightful Rosie Perez as Harrelson's girlfriend studying up to appear on *Jeopardy*.

EPILOGUE

THE TEN MINUTE MOVIE MAVEN

A maven is an authority, and becoming a movie maven is your shortcut to critical celebrity. Here's how it works: The clock starts running as the film fades to black and the end credits come up.

Minute 1:

Just think. Watch the end credits go by and try to remember three things:
• What was the director's name?
• What was the single best scene in the film?
• Who gave the best performance?

Don't analyze. Don't drive yourself crazy. Just try and come up with the answers to those three questions. Then get up and leave your seat.

Minute 2:

As you're walking out, answer the next three questions:
• Was this the most perfect movie you've ever seen in your life?
• Was it absolutely the worst film you've ever seen?
• On a line between perfection and disgraceful, where would you put this film?

You have to put it somewhere on that line. No fudging, no smearing, no double lines allowed. Is it near the bottom? Close to the top? In the middle? Some people think of a scale from 1 to 100 and pick a number. The American Film Institute likes to do that. I don't recommend shortening it (1 to 10, say) because each number is just too broad and contains too many variables. If you're going to use numbers, use 1 to 100. "That's tied for 58th," for instance, sounds better than "I give it a 6." Too much can go into that 6 for it to be meaningful. So anything above 70, say, is pretty good to great; and anything below 30 is probably a bomb. But you decide.

Minute 3:

This is a good time to suggest going someplace for ice cream or a drink. When your companion says, "So, what did you think?" you say, "Just give me a second; I'm trying to remember something." Nobody interrupts anybody who's trying to remember, and what you're trying to remember is whether or not you ever saw any other films by this director. If you're just drawing a blank, you ask your companion "What other films did this director make?" If neither of you can remember, or if you can and it turns out that this is a first film, then skip to Minute 5. Otherwise, answer these questions:

•Is this the best film you've seen by Mr./Ms. _____?
•Is it the worst?
•Where on the scale would you put it?

Here you won't use that 1 to 100 scale, of course, and some directors are pretty hard to classify. For Robert Zemeckis, for instance, you could be forced to place a film somewhere in the ether between *Who Framed Roger Rabbit?*, *Forrest Gump*, and *Contact*. But if you don't get sidetracked by the differences in subject matter, you'll see that all three are examples of overwrought hammering on stories that can't bear much weight. Or maybe you won't, but you get my point. You can see that we're narrowing things down here, focusing in more tightly.

Minute 4:

Now we'll start setting this film in context. Answer these questions:
•How is it similar to the director's other films?
•How is it different?

Don't think you have to dream up huge amounts of information and opinion here. Don't bother going deep. Just say whether it's in the same genre, or if it's a new departure.

And what you'll probably find is that most directors make films that are a lot like their other films in a lot of ways. Same theme, maybe, or same types of characters, or the same conflicts, or the same kind of humor. Stylistically you may find similarities in how this one was shot or edited, as compared with the others.

Don't go crazy with this, though. Many directors are just hired hands who got to do the film because they're friends with the star, or their agent sold them to the producer as part of a package along with the writer, or because they're cheap and available. But the ones who have a distinctive style or approach, or who write as well as direct their films, are more likely to be worth thinking about.

Minute 5:

Spend this minute thinking about the script. Here are some questions you can ask yourself:
- How many interesting characters did the writer create?
- Did the dialogue ring true? Would real people talk like that?
- Could you predict events or twists in the plot before the writer wanted you to do it?
- Would real people act the way the characters did?
- If it's a drama, do the conflicts grow out of the nature of each character, or are they just contrived and artificial?
- The best-written films, like the best novels or plays, take us emotional places we normally don't ever get to go to. We've long since suspended our disbelief and are caught up in the created work. If that's how this film made you feel, then it was terrific, right?

Minute 6:

This is your 1-minute acting analysis. If you know the actors, and have seen them before, here are your questions:
- Did the stars act exactly as you've seen them act in other films, so that they're just doing what you might call a star turn?
- Were they extending their range to try something different?
- Did you respond to the characters on the screen or to the stars themselves?

Here's an example: Johnny Depp made his initial reputation as a young man with a very boyish face and manner. By 1997, in *Donnie Brasco*, he had extended his range to play an undercover FBI agent who infiltrates the mob, with no hint of boyish mannerisms. On the other hand, Michael J. Fox played his whole career as a boyish, charming rake.

Some parts are written, or rewritten, for stars to play without stretching or straining themselves, but some stars insist on stretching themselves for every film. Sean Penn, Meryl Streep, Glenn Close, and Anthony Hopkins come to mind.

It isn't necessarily bad for an actor to play only one role. Buster Keaton and Charlie Chaplin did it quite well. But it makes each film into a vehicle for the star, and if the writer and director are trying to tell a story about real human beings it can only bring sorrow to everyone involved.

Minute 7:
For this minute, you think power. What kind of dramatic power did this film have over you? And by the way, comedies can have power as well as dramas, as long as they have emotional content as well as verbal or physical comedy. A comedy like Chaplin's *City Lights* has power because of the tramp's relationship with the blind girl and the unraveling of that relationship at the end. *When Harry Met Sally. . .* has power because it uses Billy Crystal's own wit and one-liners as insights into the defenses his character throws up around himself. So answer these questions:
  •Were you absorbed in the film or in getting the popcorn butter off your hands?
  •Did the film force you to think about implications for your own life?
  •Was there a sense of truth that you could feel about the people whose lives you saw on the screen?

Any film that has power is going to be at least pretty good on your scale, and maybe a lot more.

Minute 8:
Hit the high points. If the film wasn't unendurably dull from beginning to end it must have had some moments or characters or scenes that you liked, and maybe even loved. The 1996 comedy *Mars Attacks* was a dreadful film for a lot of reasons, but the Martians themselves were absolutely wonderful.
  •Was there any part of the film that you would enjoy reminiscing about with a friend?
  •Did you get any sense that the film had a rhythm to it, some purposeful plan that governed how the sequence of scenes was laid out, with highs and lows figured in?
Most films aren't very good, and one reason they're not is that they're flat. Flatly written, flatly directed, uninterestingly acted. Films that have high points are likely to be better than those that don't.

Minute 9:

Let's wrap it up here. Summarize Minutes 1 through 8 in your own mind. Pick and choose what appealed to you and what should be discarded, and come to a conclusion. Don't try to put everything into a neat package; it will never work, even with very bad films. Just decide on an overall response to the movie, as though you were going to deliver it to a television audience or to newspaper or magazine readers. Remember: Roger Ebert isn't perfect, and you don't have to be either.

Minute 10:

Deliver the verdict. By this time you've reached the bar or ice cream parlor and ordered, so while you're waiting is the best moment to say your piece. Your friends will be amazed at your analysis, and may even pick up the check. That'll be a sign that you've arrived.

APPENDIX

WHERE TO FIND ALL THE FILMS

Once upon a time, perhaps as far back as 1998, it was accepted that you rented your videos in VHS format from the local store, took them home to play on your VCR, and watched them on your two- or three-year-old television set. No more.

Two major changes — no, three — have revolutionized the home-viewing business. The first is the DVD, which in a size and space no larger than a CD, gives you more and better, and better-looking, film content than any VHS format could hope to do, and comes in a package that's easier to use, and more convenient, than laser disks. The second is HDTV, high-definition television, which is remaking all viewing habits as it replaces the old transmission standards with TV pictures that almost match film's fine grain for quality, and in a height-to-width format that's closer to the way movies are shot today. And the third is the proliferation of online, internet sources for almost every possible film you'd ever want to rent. Ask any internet portal for movies — and you can specify everything from horror to porno to classics to westerns — and you'll be choosing from among dozens of suppliers. Just bring your credit card.

The most complete list of sources for films I know is *Leonard Maltin's Annual Movie and Video Guide*, which is also indispensable for meeting new films, rediscovering old favorites, and reminding yourself that it was, in fact, Michelle Pfeiffer in *Charlie Chan and the Curse of the Dragon Queen*. Maltin's group of contract film-critic writers has an amazing ability to summarize any film — great, good, fair, poor, or stinking — in one thoughtful, well-written paragraph. Try it yourself some time if you think it's easy.

The best short guide to people in and around films — actors, directors, writers, producers, cinematographers, composers, designers, editors — is still *Halliwell's Filmgoer's Companion*, in its various editions. And the back of the book has some charming notes, along with everything from complete Academy Award lists to a fine bibliography of reference works to a worldwide history of film itself.

By far the best reference work for your library is David Thomson's extraordinary achievement *A Biographical Dictionary of the Cinema*. Accurate, open, opinionated, knowledgeable beyond the simply factual, Thomson's work is like having a great and thoughtful friend at your side to help you get to know the artists and their work. You can read it simply for the pleasure of encountering his perceptive writing. It's the first book you should buy, and the best in the field. I don't always agree with his judgments, but like any great critic he lays out his reasoning for you, so you can make up your own mind.

Which leads us to the question of criticism and its practitioners. Who, if anyone, can we trust? Well, ourselves, for sure. But who can enlarge our understanding, enrich our experience? Unlike some other art forms, critics of film are rarely practitioners themselves (Roger Ebert is an exception, having written three produced screenplays). Where novelists review new novels, poets review poetry, and at least substantial academic credits are required of critics of music, architecture, and the visual arts, there are no criteria for film critics. Film is probably the only art form where the amateurs[6], at best enthusiasts, are accepted as experts in the field. Does this mean that their work is inherently bad, or badly flawed? Not necessarily, but it does mean that we should not take their judgments on faith. When we listen to, say, a performance of a late Mozart symphony, we may respond viscerally, emotionally, passionately; but without at least some academic or experiential training — more than a few music lessons, for example — we'll have a hard time pinning down the architecture of the work, the decisions regarding orchestration and color, that Mozart made to give us that feeling. Similarly, it helps to know how a movie is made before we share our opinions of it with the world, or at least our viewers and readers.

The members of the French New Wave, before they were filmmakers, were, almost all of them, film critics, besotted with films and soaking up every movie that played in Paris. American films, Swedish, Italian, German,

---

[6] I use the word 'amateur' in the French sense of a lover of something, in this case film, rather than in the Yiddish sense of a *potchkyer*, a weekend tennis player or golfer. You have to be a lover of film to spend your days and nights viewing films and then writing coherent prose about each and every one of them.

Russian, Japanese, and of course French. They smoked, they drank, they talked films day and night, and they wrote endlessly about them in the film journal *Cahiers du Cinema*. Truffaut particularly was a scholar of film as well as a critic, and in the middle of his own filmmaking career found the time to interview Alfred Hitchcock for his famous book *Hitchcock/Truffaut*, in which he records their conversations about Hitchcock's entire film career.

Pauline Kael, America's legendary film critic, was not a filmmaker nor an academic, but managed and programmed a repertory cinema in Berkeley for years, writing précis and descriptions of each and every film she showed. She was omnivorous and on the evidence never forgot a thing she saw. In her career as *The New Yorker's* film critic she was able to draw on that almost-encyclopedic knowledge. Her early insistence on programming as many foreign films as domestic ones was invaluable to her work as a critic. It was a lucky break, a luxury unavailable even these days to critics outside New York or Los Angeles, who must find the time, energy, and will to screen videos of foreign or genre films outside of business hours, or travel to the big city to do it.

At any rate, the big four sources for serious film buffs are:

Movies Unlimited, 3015 Darnell Road, Philadelphia, PA 19154 phone 1-800-466-8437; www.moviesunlimited.com

Facets Video, 1517 W. Fullerton Ave., Chicago, IL 60614 phone 1-800-331-6197; www.facets.org

Home Film Festival, P.O. Box 2032, Scranton, PA 18501 phone 1-800-258-3456; www.homefilmfestival.com

Kino International, 333 W. 39th Street, New York, NY 10018 phone 1-800-562-3330; www.kino.com

Try them all, send for their catalogs, start spending money. Invite your friends to watch with you. You'll never regret it.

INDEX OF FILMS

V

W

Y

Z

ACKNOWLEDGMENTS

This book's gestation began when I was still in single digits and my mother took me regularly to the Thalia, New York's first art-house, to see films like *The Baker's Wife*, which taught me to speed-read subtitles. It progressed through my Bergman years, flowered when my first documentary film was selected for screening at the Robert Flaherty Film Seminar, and took on a life of its own when my children began criticizing my reviews. Once, my then-8-year-old son took it upon himself to write the television station attacking my putdown of *Roger Rabbit*. The news anchor read his letter on the air.

So my thanks must go first to Glenna Glatzer, who at 94 still walks over to the Lincoln Center Cinemas once or twice a week and calls me with her opinions, and to my most patient and amazingly supportive wife Mary Ann Murphy, who always encouraged me to write it. I'm particularly indebted to her for the line: 'Irony is what doesn't play in Spokane.' I'm grateful to my three children, Gaby, Jessica and Nick, who keep me on my critical toes by vehemently disagreeing with me; and to my partners on the weekly public radio show *Movies 101*, Dan Webster, Leonard Oakland, and Marty Demarest.

Most specifically I thank Tony Flinn, my brilliant editor, who not only has impeccable taste but knows how to improve everything from a clause to a chapter with just the slightest touch of an email. Amazing.

Some invaluable research assistance came from Kristine Krueger of the National Film Information Service at the Motion Picture Academy, and from the work of critics and historians who are mentioned in the text. All errors, though, are exclusively mine.

One chapter of this book appeared, in slightly different form, in the online magazine Salon.com.

ROBERT GLATZER

Robert Glatzer is a film writer and critic in Spokane, Washington, where he hosts the weekly public radio show "Movies 101" and is the film critic for two NPR stations. A former film director in New York City, his films have been award-winning festival selections around the world. He has taught film in New York at the School of Visual Arts, and in Spokane at Eastern Washington University. He currently directs Spokane's Northwest Film Festival.